TUNES

A COMIC BOOK HISTORY
OF ROCK AND ROLL

EDITED BY VINCENT BRUNNER

Preface by Mathias Malzieu

UNIVERSE

WARNING

A preface by Mathias Malzieu

Dear reader: before throwing yourself body and soul into this giant vortex, here are a few instructions for use.

If you assume the responsibility of reading this manual, you may feel a surge of adrenaline, the kind that could take over your entire body. It might even make you dance—and in front of everyone, too. The first symptoms will be as follows: lascivious undulating of the pelvis from left to right, puckering of the mouth into a soft frown like Mick Jagger, and shamanic hooting that will make you sound like a werewolf, escaped from some underground zoo.

Please note: delving into this book may inspire you to skip the weekend you'd planned with your uncle and drive across Death Valley in a beat-up Corvette instead. Even if you only speed around your neighborhood in a pedal go-kart, you'll still feel like a goddamned pioneer. Because the treasures you'll find in these comic strips are the very stories and legends of rock and roll at its wildest.

Over the course of your journey, a full mini-bar will be at your disposal, courtesy of Elvis Presley's ghost, decked out in leather like he was in his '68 comeback special.

On the menu: thinly sliced Pixies with a drizzle of Nirvana, and a hint of a tidal wave; some crisp Nick Drake and an electrifying scoop of AC/DC, and other blood-red pastries, with a dab of White Stripes. This is the most danceable book in the world. Listen to it, read it, sing it, look at it. Maybe you can even eat it. But read it first. A treasure map—they call it a table of contents—will be provided a takeoff, even if you're only in a go-kart. Here you'll find a clear list of addresses for the ghost towns haunted by rock and roll's most memorable representatives, dead and alive.

So take a walk through the garden carefully grown by PJ Harvey, learn the xylophone by playing on an imaginary skeleton with the Clash, and go out with a bang with Joy Division in the euphemistic cemetery of Ian Curtis and his classy crows. If you bring some good Irish whiskey, they might even whistle a few notes of 'She's Lost Control' for you. You'll also find Iggy Pop in a colorful adaptation of *Alice in Wonderland*, along with a no-less colorful text describing his journey to Crimson Country, which lives on today. Follow the paths of our icons, cradled by the lullaby of a hissing mic. Rock and roll and comic books overlap one another and expand. Rock singers all have a bit of superhero in them, in their onstage extravagance, in the way they move, and in their chronic inability to adapt to normal life and society. In rock, there are tribes, which we call "groups"—underground societies that swarm with fear and joy beneath our very feet. While Iggy Pop is (perfectly portrayed in these pages as the rabbit-iguana in *Alice in Wonderland*, Nick Cave could very well have been Batman. Of course, the mask would be hot to wear during concerts, and I don't think the Batmobile is as good as an old white van for carrying equipment. But, in his melancholy, which he claimed and transformed into a vital force both in his albums and on stage, Nick Cave could be one of Batman's strange cousins. What's more, PJ Harvey would make a first-rate Catwoman by his side. There's another bizarre parallel between rock singers and superheroes: Jack White might as well have been Johnny Depp's double. Depp was Edward Scissorhands, but White focused his magic on the tips of his fingers, which seem to become living guitar slides. Unearthing some of the most burning blues from deep-down Mississippi, he's a truly super superhero, who reignited public interest in hidden treasures like Dolly Parton's 'Jolene' (don't laugh—that song is so beautiful, it's scary). But don't try and make me believe Elton John could be Spiderman, because listening to him sing in a form-fitting Spidey-suit, you'd quickly realize how impossible that would be.

We're not going to let the merry-go-round just stop: as soon as you close this book, you'll want to jump back on. It's already time to head back, to continue exploring. It's time to get ready for the big, fun leap. Load the i-Deck onto the back seat of your go-kart, grab something to eat and drink, and nothing can stop you. If you don't have a go-kart or a record player, that won't stop you either; you can fly over the Rockies right from your bed. Lean out, fall, and have a blast.

Mathias Malzieu is the charismatic lead singer of the rock group Dionysos. He's also the author of Maintenant qu'il fait tout le temps nuit sur toi (Flammarion, 2005; J'ai lu, 2006) and La Méchanique du Coeur [The Boy with the Cuckoo-Clock Heart] (Chatto & Windus, 2009).

First published in the United States of America
in 2010 by
Universe Publishing
A Division of Rizzoli International Publications, Inc.
300 Park Avenue South
New York, NY 10010
www.rizzoliusa.com

ISBN: 978-0-7893-2200-5
Library of Congress Catalog Control Number:
2010931051

Originally published in French by
Flammarion, Paris, 2009
Flammarion editor: Gaelle Lassée
Original design by Serge Bilous
Translated into English by Molly Stevens
Universe design and English lettering by
Chris McDonnell
Printed in the United States of America

The Rolling Stones
MORVANDIAU
32

The Kinks
LUC CORNILLON
42

Janis Joplin
CATEL & PARINGAUX - 50

DAVID BOWIE
NINE ANTICO
78

Elton John
CHARLES BERBERIAN
86

LED ZEPPELIN
KILLOFFER - 94

AC/DC
APPOLLO-BRÜNO
132

Blondie
STANISLAS GROS
124

RAMONES
SÉBASTIEN LUMINEAU
140

new Order
NYLSO - 174

NICK CAVE
LAURE DEL PINO
182

METALLICA
RIAD SATTOUF - 190

NIRVANA
GUILLAUME BOUZARD
218

the WHITE STRIPES
MATHIEU SAPIN - 224

lcd sound system
LUZ - 232

First a torrid rocker, then a chaste priest. Before staging the occasional comeback—defrocked—Richard Penniman has definitely had many lives, from fiery lights to priestly faith, from fame to refuge. But his career could have ended in 1957 without tarnishing his image as a rock-and-roll pioneer. No matter what he does, history will remember Penniman as Little Richard, the hysterical madman with impressive hair (a pompadour some six inches high) and exuberant moves, a role he played between 1955 and 1957 with a flamboyance that would never be matched. During those two years, Little Richard never stopped recording—it was if he were in a trance—and completed more than fifty songs. Some of them, like 'Long Tall Sally,' 'Lucille,' or the salacious 'Tutti Frutti,' changed the world, electrified bodies, and charged libidos and minds (just ask the Beatles). Young people all over the world were initiated into rock this way (it was like losing their virginity), and their aphrodisiacs were a gay rocker and Elvis Presley. Only Chuck Berry, another black rocker, can boast of having so shaped the codes of the genre (including the guitar intro) and of having provided future generations with such a repertoire (including 'Johnny B. Goode,' 'Roll over Beethoven,' 'Maybellene,' 'Memphis,' and others). At first, Richard's destiny wasn't so rebellious: he grew up in Macon, Georgia, in a deeply religious environment and quickly joined the church choir to start singing gospel. But the young Richard was also tempted by less holy pleasures, although they didn't seem incompatible with his faith. After all, his father, a preacher and the head of a family of twelve, was bringing home money that came from selling distilled alcohol. When the singer Lloyd Price, who made 'Stagger Lee' popular, first recommended Richard to Specialty, an R&B record label, Richard was performing blues songs in a classic style and wasn't that impressive. It didn't suit him or his tempo (which, deep down, he preferred fast). Then, during

PLAYLIST

1 Little Richard's Boogie (1955)
2 Tutti Frutti (1957)
3 Ready Teddy (1957)
4 Slippin' and Slidin' (1957)
5 Long Tall Sally (1957)
6 Miss Ann (1957)
7 Oh Why? (1957)
8 Rip It Up (1957)
9 Jenny, Jenny (1957)
10 Keep a Knockin' (1958)
11 By the Light of the Silvery Moon (1958)
12 Good Golly Miss Molly (1958)
13 Ooh ! My Soul (1958)
14 The Girl Can't Help It (1958)
15 Lucille (1958)
16 Directly From My Heart to You (1959)
17 Kansas City (1959)
18 I'm Just a Lonely Guy (1959)
19 Bama Lama Bama (1964)
20 I Don't Know What You've Got (But It's Got Me) (1965)

LITTLE

SELECTED DISCOGRAPHY

The Very Best Of (Specialty)
With Little Richard, it's best to go with an anthology. This one has most of the explosive sexual hits of his early and best years. Another compilation, *The Georgia Peach*, not as recent, also offers a very good selection in chronological order.

Vincent ('Be Bop a Lula') and Eddie Cochrane ('Something Else'), other pioneers, and also the sizzling Jayne Mansfield in *The Girl Can't Help It*. His omnipresence clashed with the blackout that came at the end of 1957. In the middle of a successful tour, his original dilemma resurfaced: preach the sacred or sing the profane in the form of rock and roll? His collaborator, Jerry Lee Lewis,

FIRST A TORRID ROCKER, THEN A CHASTE PRIEST, RICHARD PENNIMAN HAS DEFINITIVELY HAD MANY LIVES

A story by
Blexbolex

a killer piano player, also had the same scruples about playing the "devil's music." Because of an airplane scare (a sign?), Little Richard decided to step away from the spotlight and become a seventh-day preacher like his father. While believing that Christ would return, he also planned a comeback—first as a well-behaved gospel singer. But then he bit into the apple of rock. In the mid-sixties, a new generation of English youth saw him as a godfather—praise well

RICHARD

BORN IN 1935

deserved—and got their training by playing his songs. During the 1960s, he crossed paths with future stars: in Hamburg, he shared the stage of the Star Club with the Beatles, who were just learning the ropes. He toured with the Rolling Stones and hired an unknown Jimi Hendrix as a guitarist. In the decades that followed, he wavered between theology and profitable concerts, forever disappearing and coming back to tour with other rock legends, like Chuck Berry and Jerry Lee Lewis. Despite time's passing, these songs still have the same electrifying power. Just witness the effect 'Lucille' has on Blexbolex's hero!

a break when the mics were off, Richard let loose on a baby grand, playing an energetic tune that revealed his true nature: showy, sexy, even completely obscene. Starting with a thundering "A-wop-bop-aloo-bop-a-lop-bam-boom," the bawdy song 'Tutti Frutti' celebrated the perfect pairing of boogie-woogie piano and rhythm-and-blues brass. From that point on, Little Richard would be everywhere, making the black R&B charts, but also the white pop charts. He was even on screen, starring with Gene

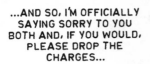

...AND SO, I'M OFFICIALLY SAYING SORRY TO YOU BOTH AND, IF YOU WOULD, PLEASE DROP THE CHARGES...

LET'S SAY WE'RE WILLING TO ACCEPT, BUT DON'T EVEN THINK ABOUT STARTING UP AGAIN.

YOU SHOULD HAVE UNDERSTOOD THAT IT WAS OVER, BERNARD. WE DON'T LIKE BEING LIKE THIS, YOU KNOW.

YOU'RE SICK!

WHAT PUSHED ME OVER THE EDGE WAS WHEN YOU WERE CLINGING TO THE DOORMAT SCREAMING, BUCK NAKED. WE HAD TO CALL THE COPS TO PEEL YOU OFF! HAVE YOU NO SENSE OF DECENCY?

SORRY.

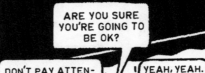

ARE YOU SURE YOU'RE GOING TO BE OK?

DON'T PAY ATTENTION TO HIM. I JUST WANT HIM TO GET OUT OF HERE!

YEAH, YEAH. IT'LL BE FINE.

FAREWELL, BERNARD.

FAREWELL, LUCILLE.

WHAT IS THIS?! DAMN, I DON'T BELIEVE IT. SHE LEFT HER CLOTHES!

WHAT A SOW!

WHAT WAS SHE THINKING? DO I LOOK LIKE A LUGGAGE RACK?!

WELL, TAKE A LOOK AT WHAT I'M GOING TO DO WITH YOUR SHIT!!

SNIF SNIF

LUCILLE?

With Presley, objectivity is out. 'Rocket 88,' a song written by Ike Turner, who was then married to Tina—and which became popular in 1951 with Bill Haley's harder version—stylistically marked the birth of that strange thing called rock and roll. But history tends to prefer symbols to exactitude. It remembers moments. For example, when an electrician with dreams of singing had some fun with two musicians he hardly knew and let loose on an old blues tune. What was just a studio session with no future became a myth: the day in 1954 when Elvis Presley, along with Scotty Moore on guitar and Bill Black on bass, played a carefree version of 'That's All Right.' A few months before, a well-groomed Elvis had gone to see Sam Phillips, the man at Sun Records, to record a four-track acetate, supposedly to be a present for his mother. Born into a family of modest means, he was drawn early on to all the music that played on the radio, from white country to black rhythm and blues, bluegrass, and gospel. 'That's All Right' is what fueled the fire and cast the spell. Then Elvis broke ground and cleared the way, starting a revolution with his buddies without even knowing it. They tried out the radio circuit, touring and playing for small country and western stations. The country began to tremble. On stage, Elvis electrified the crowd with his eccentric and disheveled look, his dance moves, and his suggestive pelvic thrusts, forcing television stations to film him only above the waist. Prudish America wanted to extinguish this devilish pyromaniac, but Elvis, an innocent pretty boy, lay his charisma and sex appeal onto a wave of hysterical young women. It was all magnified when Tom Parker, known as the Colonel, an entertainment impresario, became his manager, and used television as a launching pad. At that point, Elvis left the small label Sun Records—along with Johnny Cash, Carl Perkins ('Blue Suede Shoes'), and Jerry Lee Lewis—for the biggest label there was at the time, RCA.

A story by Ruppert and Mulot

ELVIS PRESLEY
1935 – 1977

By 1956 he was already an icon, a legend, with a tall stack of gold albums under his belt (thanks to 'Heartbreak Hotel,' 'Don't be Cruel,' and other songs). Then Parker built an acting career for his protégé. He introduced him to Hollywood so that he could be on both scenes— Elvis would make soundtracks. Burning through three movies a year, his filmography was growing

ON STAGE, ELVIS ELECTRIFIED THE CROWD WITH HIS ECCENTRIC AND DISHEVELED LOOK, HIS DANCE MOVES, AND HIS SUGGESTIVE PELVIC THRUSTS

by the minute. It was an optical illusion: the feature-length films he appeared in were mostly insignificant, mediocre. Unaware that he was a guinea pig, Elvis invented all the tropes of rock star life, tearing through each one. At thirty-three, he made an impressive comeback, thanks to a televised program on NBC. In 1969 he went back to performing, first for a series of shows in Las Vegas, then for a full U.S. tour. But the young rocker had become a chubby Sinatra-style crooner who was less exciting to girls than to their mothers. Because of his bad eating habits (the King of junk food?), his addiction to pills, and his overacting, Elvis became a caricature of what he once was. Luckily, his voice was still there. The last symbolic episode: once the embodiment of freedom and rebellion in the mid-fifties, Elvis was a rock-and-roll dinosaur by the time the English punks raged onto the stage. In the song '1977,' the Clash sang that they didn't want Elvis or the Beatles or the Rolling Stones anymore.

Coincidence: on August 16 of that same year, Elvis passed away at Graceland, his home in Memphis. But between remasters and unreleased songs, he's the bestselling dead singer in the world. Ruppert and Mulot take a look at the career of this living dead man.

PLAYLIST

1 That's All Right (1954)
2 Blue Moon (1954)
3 Mystery Train (1955)
4 Heartbreak Hotel (1956)
5 Hound Dog (1956)
6 Don't Be Cruel (1956)
7 Love Me Tender (1956)
8 All Shook Up (1957)
9 Jailhouse Rock (1957)
10 King Creole (1958)
11 Crawfish (1958)
12 It's Now or Never (1960)
13 Can't Help Falling in Love (1961)
14 (You're the) Devil in Disguise (1963)
15 Viva Las Vegas (1963)
16 Suspicious Minds (1969)
17 In the Ghetto (1969)
18 Always on my Mind (1972)
19 My Way (1977)
20 A Little Less Conversation, JXL remix (2002)

SELECTED DISCOGRAPHY

Sunrise (1999)
All the Sun Records recordings, the start of it all.

Elvis Presley (1956)
The first album from the Sun years.

From Elvis in Memphis (1969)
The King, mature.

Elvis : 30 #1 Hits (2002)
Thirty hits, no less.

The Complete Million Dollar Quartet (2006)
The impromptu 1958 jam session at the Sun Records Studios with Carl Perkins, Johnny Cash, and Jerry Lee Lewis.

basements and clubs in Hamburg. But it allowed them to make a name for themselves in Mersey beat (the movement named after the Liverpool river). Their efforts paid off: as early as 1963, and with their first album, Beatlemania exploded in England, sparking riots. The group's schedule—between concerts and radio and TV engagements—got crazy. Spellbound, Britain celebrated its heroes. The band's sexual energy drove young women wild, but their nice student looks reassured their parents.

The following year, the Beatles traveled on tour around the world several times over and went to the United States, drawing in more than seventy million television viewers when they appeared on the *Ed Sullivan Show* and starred in their first movie. Their concerts were now taking place in stadiums and produced such ghastly

BEFORE BECOMING MASTERS OF POP MUSIC, WHOSE INFLUENCE IS STILL MIND-BLOWING, LIVERPOOL'S FOUR SONS WERE ROCK STUDENTS WHO LEARNED THEIR PROFESSION THE HARD WAY

The Beatles have been compared to the Rolling Stones for decades. It's so persistent that any rock enthusiast will feel obliged to choose a camp. The rivalry is completely artificial (the bands went to the same parties and helped each other out in the studio) and masks musical developments that can't be compared. While the Stones, led by Jagger and Richards, continue to fight against the ravages of time, the Beatles were only around for some ten years. But they covered a lot of ground during that decade: the fits and starts of the rock-and-roll circus, exhausting tours, sudden and incredible fame, the chart chase, brilliant experiments, and then internal friction before the final blow.

Before becoming masters of pop music, whose influence is still mind-blowing, Liverpool's four sons—John Lennon, Paul McCartney, George Harrison, and Ringo Starr (who replaced the drummer Pete Best, who didn't fit)—were rock students who learned their profession the hard way, playing at a relentless pace in stuffy

hysteria in fans that they slowly started to pull away from performing. Their albums, however, were more than just collections of quickly compiled hits. Recording studios, especially Abbey Road in London, became more and more important to their experimentation. Having already obeyed the rules established by the music industry, the Beatles came into their own and listened only to their own ideas and ambitions. Brian Wilson, the brilliant brain behind the Beach Boys, was both jealous and full of admiration. And so they approached *Sgt. Pepper* as if they were writing a book, spending seven hundred hours recording it—a far cry from the thirteen-hour session that produced their first album! Not only did the group significantly expand their sound palette—this is when George Harrison picked up the Indian sitar—but they played along with their recording as it played in reverse. They were inventing new sounds, following Paul McCartney's lead, introducing avant-garde ideas into pop. Behind its unstoppable melody, the

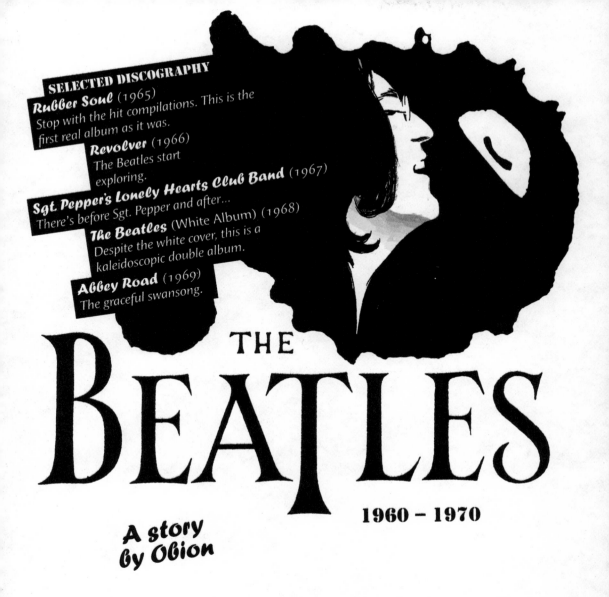

THE BEATLES

1960 – 1970

A story by Obion

single 'All You Need is Love,' with its references to Bach, Glenn Miller, and 'She Loves You,' paved the way for the kind of sampling that's so popular in today's hip hop and techno. With help from drugs—marijuana (they smoked a joint in the bathroom at Buckingham Palace) and LSD, among others—the four pushed the artistic envelope, composing 'Tomorrow Never Knows' as early as 1966, which was based on the psychedelic manual written by the famous LSD champion, Timothy Leary. After the tumultuous but fruitful creation of the brilliant *White Album*, which inspired Obion's work here, each member was pulled away from the group. John Lennon sacrificed the Beatles for his love for Yoko Ono before heading down a peace-loving, anti-establishment road ('Imagine'). Paul McCartney soon launched a solo career. George Harrison turned toward the East and transcendental meditation, and Ringo Starr partied. The murder of Lennon in 1980 and Harrison's less violent death in 2001 shattered all hope of seeing the Beatles reunited one day. They provided pop music with an endless repertoire of songs (see the hundreds of versions of 'Yesterday') and—from Blur to the Red Hot Chili Peppers, from David Bowie to Franz Ferdinand—they have an ever-growing list of disciples.

Two English students meet and talk about the blues on a suburban train, form a cover band, get a manager, play like rebels, drive crowds wild, write generational hymns without a second thought, fill stadiums, and become icons that have even inspired movie directors (Jean-Luc Godard's *Sympathy for the Devil*, Robert Frank's *Cocksucker Blues*—banned for thirty years—and Martin Scorsese's *Shine a Light*). The story of these two students, Mick Jagger and Keith Richards, who, after sharing blues albums, changed many peoples' lives (even beyond their bandmates Brian Jones, Bill Wyman, Charlie Watts, Mick Taylor, and Ron Wood), is synonymous with the story of rock and roll.

In the right place at the right time, the Stones shot up to the ambassador level of the cultural and sexual revolution of the 1960s. The Stones' manager, Andrew Oldham, played a key role in their career. By buying copies of the first albums of his protégés himself, he helped them climb the charts and developed their bad boy, messy look, selling them as the group parents hate (hence the headline: "Would you let your daughter marry a Rolling Stone?"). Although the goal was to distinguish them from the Beatles, who seemed more like perfect sons-in-law, the Stones owed one of their first hits to them. John Lennon and Paul McCartney actually went to their studio to teach them 'I Wanna Be Your Man.' Persuaded by Oldham, Jagger and Richards then started composing their own tunes so as not to be so dependent on covers.

A story by Morvandiau

In their early years, they were the scrawny disciples of American bluesmen and rhythm-and-blues artists, and helped promote them in Europe (Bo Diddley, Slim Harpo, and Muddy Waters among them). Starting in 1965, Jagger and Richards began writing more and more memorable songs like 'The Last Time,' '(I Can't Get No) Satisfaction,' and dozens of others. But that didn't stop them from continuing to pay homage to blues heroes like Robert Johnson. Take for example their sublime cover of 'Love in Vain' (from 1936) on *Let It Bleed* (1969),

THE STONES SHOT UP TO THE AMBASSADOR LEVEL OF THE CULTURAL AND SEXUAL REVOLUTION OF THE 1960S

which inspired the comic artist Morvandiau in these pages. When the Jagger-Richards duo took control of the group, Brian Jones, the angelic blond guitarist, was more or less the direct victim. He was the leader before getting in over his head and becoming a burden to the others. He was also at the center of the legendary drama that unfolded in 1969. The year after the group expressed its 'Sympathy for the Devil,' the Stones let Jones go. He had become a bloated caricature of himself. A few days later he was buried. The band played in his honor in Hyde Park in London before a crowd of 500,000. Later that same year, during another free concert in Altamont, California, death came knocking again. This time, a member of the Hell's Angels hired as security stabbed a fan, who was also armed.

During the 1970s, Ron Wood, a party friend and the guitarist for the Faces, stepped in for Mick Taylor, who had replaced Brian Jones. The Stones became a huge rock-and-roll circus, with adoring fans. As for Keith Richards, he stuck with the hard drugs (despite the fact that his friend, the country rock singer Gram Parsons, died of an overdose in 1973). In 1977 he was arrested by the Canadian police for possession of cocaine and heroin. Gradually, the relationship between the two leaders deteriorated, and Mick Jagger attempted to launch a solo career (without success). The self-nicknamed Glimmer Twins were reconciled in the 1980s. Since then, the group—without Bill Wyman, who quit—have been performing regularly in juicy worldwide tours led by Jagger, now a sexagenarian rocker still in top shape and insolent form.

The Rolling Stones

FORMED IN 1962

SELECTED DISCOGRAPHY

Aftermath (1966)
The first album consisting of only Jagger-Richards songs.

Beggars Banquet (1968)
The perfect balance between bluesy roots and rock-and-roll energy.

Let It Bleed (1969)
A few months after the death of Brian Jones, a literally bloody album.

Sticky Fingers (1971)
A collection of sexual and dark songs, with a cover by Andy Warhol.

Exile on Main Street (1972)
The Stones' only double album, dark and alluring.

PLAYLIST

1 (I Can't Get No) Satisfaction (1965)
2 Play with Fire (1965)
3 Paint It Black (1966)
4 Under my Thumb (1966)
5 Let's Spend the Night Together (1967)
6 Ruby Tuesday (1967)
7 She's a Rainbow (1967)
8 Jumpin' Jack Flash (1968)
9 Sympathy for the Devil (1968)
10 Street Fighting Man (1968)
11 Honky Tonk Women (1969)
12 Gimme Shelter (1969)
13 You Can't Always Get What You Want (1969)
14 Brown Sugar (1971)
15 Wild Horses (1971)
16 Tumbling Dice (1972)
17 Angie (1973)
18 Miss You (1978)
19 Beast of Burden (1978)
20 Start Me Up (1981)

LOVE IN VAIN

(Written and composed by Robert Johnson, recorded on June 20, 1937. Covered by The Rolling Stones on the album Let it Bleed, 1969.)

KEITH RICHARDS STARTS WITH AN EVEN CADENCE OF ARPEGGIOS AND GLISSANDI ON HIS ACOUSTIC GUITAR. THE STEADY RHYTHM AND SPARE MEANS SET UP THE SOUND FOR A SENSITIVE (RE)PERFORMANCE. THE FIRST TIME HE HEARD ROBERT JOHNSON'S SUBTLE—AND SOLO— SONG, THE PIRATE-FACED MUSICIAN WONDERED WHO THE SECOND GUITARIST WAS.

Well, I followed her to the station with a suitcase in my hand
Yeah, I followed her to the station with a suitcase in my hand

MICK JAGGER SLIPS IN WITH A DELICATE VOICE AS THE FLOW OF THE PIECE BUILDS. A FEW SLIDES ON THE GUITAR, HIGH AND AIRY, ARE RELEASED INTO SPACE.

wow, it's hard to tell, it's hard to tell but all your loves in vain

TODAY THE STONES FILL STADIUMS AND HAVE GENERATED MUSICIANS INSPIRED TO BE ERSATZ CONFORMISTS. THE FAKE BAD BOYS—THEIR IMAGE WAS INVENTED TO CONTRAST THE BEATLES—ORIGINALLY BUILT THEIR ROCK ON COVERS AND TRADITIONAL SONGS. THE REBELS BECAME PART OF A STORY. AND WASN'T IT KEITH RICHARDS WHO SAID: "POP MUSICIANS ARE PEOPLE WHO WANT TO PLAY ROCK BECAUSE THEY DON'T KNOW HOW TO PLAY THE BLUES"?

When the train come in the station, I looked her in the eye

AND LET'S BE FRANK, AREN'T THE BLUES ALWAYS THE SAME? MY FIVE-YEAR-OLD DAUGHTER, SHE MAKES PICASSOS, RIGHT? THE STRIPPED-DOWN FORM OF BLUES, OF THE BLUES, DOESN'T ALLOW FOR MUCH SHOWING OFF, BLUFFING, OR PRETENDING. WHAT'S LEFT IS WORK, PERSONALITY, AND IMAGINATION. CHARLIE WATTS' UNIQUE, ENERGETIC, AND SUBTLE SWING ON THE DRUMS IS ALL HIS OWN.

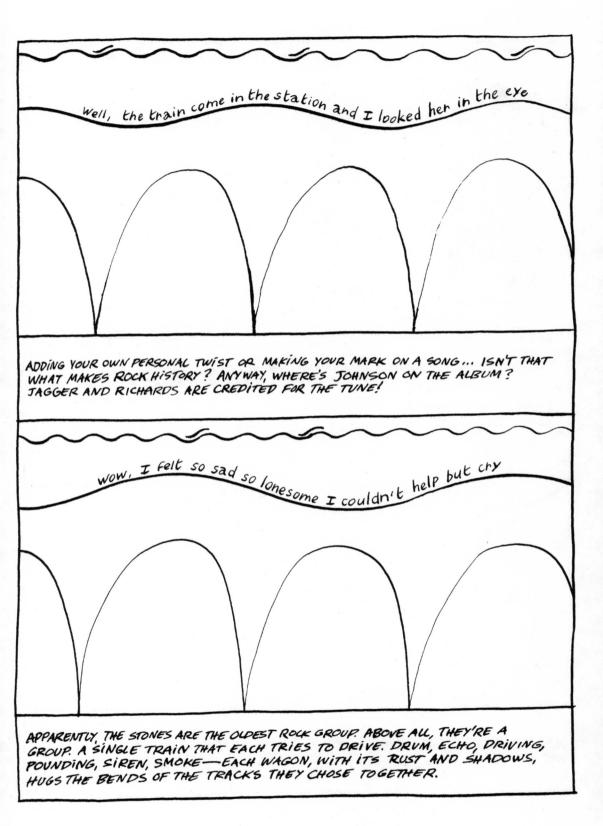

well, the train come in the station and I looked her in the eye

ADDING YOUR OWN PERSONAL TWIST OR MAKING YOUR MARK ON A SONG... ISN'T THAT WHAT MAKES ROCK HISTORY? ANYWAY, WHERE'S JOHNSON ON THE ALBUM? JAGGER AND RICHARDS ARE CREDITED FOR THE TUNE!

wow, I felt so sad so lonesome I couldn't help but cry

APPARENTLY, THE STONES ARE THE OLDEST ROCK GROUP. ABOVE ALL, THEY'RE A GROUP. A SINGLE TRAIN THAT EACH TRIES TO DRIVE. DRUM, ECHO, DRIVING, POUNDING, SIREN, SMOKE—EACH WAGON, WITH ITS RUST AND SHADOWS, HUGS THE BENDS OF THE TRACKS THEY CHOSE TOGETHER.

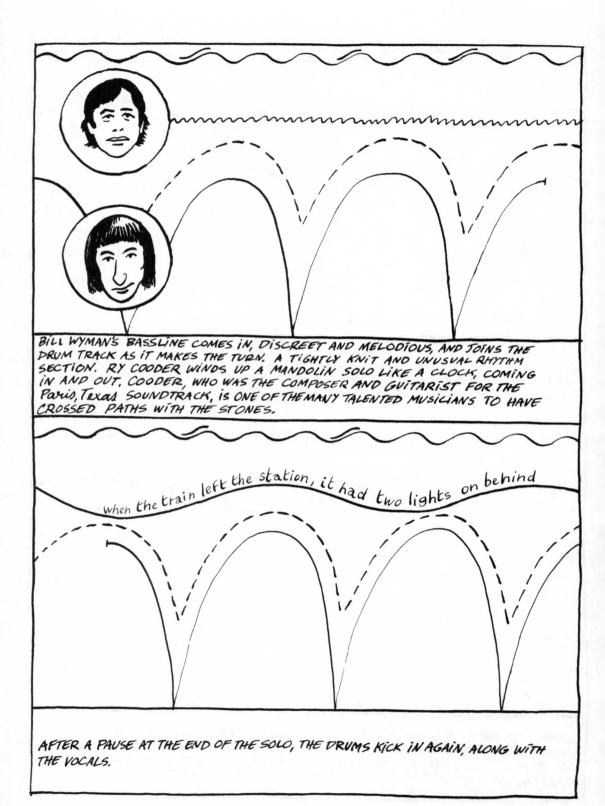

BILL WYMAN'S BASSLINE COMES IN, DISCREET AND MELODIOUS, AND JOINS THE DRUM TRACK AS IT MAKES THE TURN. A TIGHTLY KNIT AND UNUSUAL RHYTHM SECTION. RY COODER WINDS UP A MANDOLIN SOLO LIKE A CLOCK, COMING IN AND OUT. COODER, WHO WAS THE COMPOSER AND GUITARIST FOR THE Paris, Texas SOUNDTRACK, IS ONE OF THE MANY TALENTED MUSICIANS TO HAVE CROSSED PATHS WITH THE STONES.

when the train left the station, it had two lights on behind

AFTER A PAUSE AT THE END OF THE SOLO, THE DRUMS KICK IN AGAIN, ALONG WITH THE VOCALS.

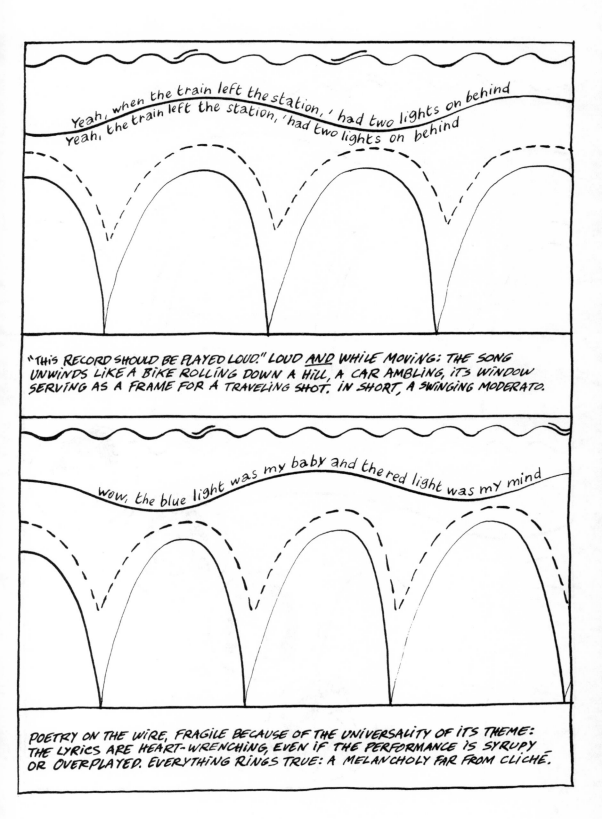

Yeah, when the train left the station, 'had two lights on behind

Yeah, the train left the station, 'had two lights on behind

"THIS RECORD SHOULD BE PLAYED LOUD." LOUD AND WHILE MOVING: THE SONG UNWINDS LIKE A BIKE ROLLING DOWN A HILL, A CAR AMBLING, ITS WINDOW SERVING AS A FRAME FOR A TRAVELING SHOT. IN SHORT, A SWINGING MODERATO.

wow, the blue light was my baby and the red light was my mind

POETRY ON THE WIRE, FRAGILE BECAUSE OF THE UNIVERSALITY OF ITS THEME: THE LYRICS ARE HEART-WRENCHING, EVEN IF THE PERFORMANCE IS SYRUPY OR OVERPLAYED. EVERYTHING RINGS TRUE: A MELANCHOLY FAR FROM CLICHÉ.

To explain why his group was not as successful as the Rolling Stones, Ray Davies, almost the only singer and composer for the Kinks, points to how easy it is for Mick Jagger to promote himself, a talent Ray doesn't have. Less exuberant than the Stones and the Beatles, the Kinks maintained their image as ordinary Englishmen and supremely talented craftsmen with little charisma. The Kinks weren't exactly reckless rockers. Of the bands of their generation, from the 1960s' "British Invasion," the Kinks are the only group not to have lost any of their members. Ray; his brother, Dave, the guitarist; and their band had a reputation for being drunks. But they didn't do drugs. In the late 1960s, when they were persona non grata for a few years in the United States, it wasn't because of some clash with the authorities or because of heroin charges; it was because of an obscure concert problem having to do with a labor union.

A story by Luc Cornillon

The KINKS

FORMED IN 1963

SELECTED DISCOGRAPHY
Face to Face (1966)
Sophisticated songs about England in the 1960s.

Something Else (1967)
The best kind of soft Britpop.

The Village Green Preservation Society (1968)
A nostalgic statement as finale.

Arthur (1969)
Delectable concept with a second title: "or the Decline and Fall of the British Empire."

Starting from the same place as their aforementioned countrymen, the Kinks did have tumultuous beginnings. The second single recorded by the Ravens (their first name) only sold a few hundred copies, but the next one, 'You Really Got Me,' had instant teenage sex appeal, and became a classic. The irresistible formula, which laid down the foundation for hard rock, was a rough guitar riff, loud chords, and a raw sound that Dave obtained by slashing his amp with a razor. When they became popular, Ray, who until that point had no ambitions as a composer, began to realize the potential his songs had. His talent for writing lyrics had been little exploited, but was soon tapped. Because they couldn't perform in the States—a big gap for the group—Ray became more and more insular. Nevertheless, many Kinks songs have been made into French versions, as Luc Cornillon points out.

After singing about his neighborhood in his first songs, the Kinks' lead singer turned a sometimes-bittersweet eye to his roots. He sang tenderly about an innocent and traditional England on the verge of disappearing, an England that belonged to the middle classes of cricket matches and afternoon tea. Without being sentimental, Ray stirred up the same emotions we feel when we look through photo albums, and explored an unusual question for pop music—how to deal with one's past. He therefore could have been unfairly seen as too conservative. This is why *The Village Green Preservation Society* was such a failure at the time, even though it's so musically rich. Influenced by British music hall and folk music, his ideas were brilliantly inventive, in spite of the album's traditional derivations. 'Lola,' a hit sustained by a charming chorus, tells of the romance between a young man and a transvestite.

Unfortunately, their luck ran out in the 1970s, when the Kinks were putting out rock operas that were hit or miss. The group traveled down a rocky road, which the band's original bass guitarist blames in hindsight on infighting. The relationship between the brothers was often explosive, especially because, with regard to composing, Ray kept all the control. What's ironic is that neither brother ever succeeded on his own. In the mid-1990s, the Kinks became popular again, and were a major reference on the Britpop scene. From Damon Albarn of Blur to Jarvis Cocker of Pulp, all the young songwriters of the time built their song lists based on these roots. As for the Kinks, there's still a hovering possibility of a reunion.

THE LEAD SINGER OF THE KINKS SANG TENDERLY ABOUT AN INNOCENT AND TRADITIONAL ENGLAND ON THE VERGE OF DISAPPEARING

PLAYLIST

1 You Really Got Me (1964)
2 Stop Your Sobbing (1964)
3 All Day and All of the Night (1965)
4 Tired of Waiting for You (1965)
5 Till the End of the Day (1965)
6 Where Have all the Good Times Gone (1965)
7 Dedicated Follower of Fashion (1966)
8 Rosie Won't You Please Come Home (1966)
9 Dandy (1966)
10 Sunny Afternoon (1966)
11 I'm Not Like Everybody Else (1966)
12 Dead End Street (1966)
13 David Watts (1967)
14 Death of a Clown (1967)
15 Waterloo Sunset (1967)
16 Picture Book (1968)
17 Days (1968)
18 Shangri-La (1969)
19 Lola (1970)
20 Low Budget (1979)

THE KINKS IN FRANCE!

BY LUC CORNILLON

THERE YOU ARE!

MUSWELL HILL

PE records

HELLO! I'M HERE TO TALK TO YOU ABOUT THE KINKS! THE THIRD BIGGEST ENGLISH ROCK BAND AFTER THE BEATLES AND STONES.

IN 1964 RAY AND DAVE DAVIES FROM MUSWELL HILL (NORTH LONDON) FORMED THE KINKS WITH TWO OTHER MATES.

RAY DAVIES

DAVE DAVIES

PETE QUAIFE

MICK AVORY

IN THEIR RED RIDING JACKETS, FRILLY SHIRTS, AND BOOTS, THEY WERE ALWAYS IMPECCABLE!

THEY BEGAN THEIR CAREER PERFORMING SOME OF THE MOST THUNDERING SONGS OF THE EARLY 1960S, AND LATER CREATED UNFORGETTABLE MELODIES AND THE MOST JOYFUL TUNES ON THE POP SCENE. BASICALLY THEY WERE ALWAYS BOUND TO WIN OVER THE FRENCH.

UNFORGETTABLE SONGS LIKE 'YOU REALLY GOT ME' AND 'ALL DAY AND ALL OF THE NIGHT'...

GIRL! YOU REALLY GOT ME NOW

TOU DOU DOU DOUM

TOU DOU DOU DOUM

The KINKS

FRENCH AUDIENCES WERE QUICK TO APPRECIATE THESE ENERGETIC SONGS... WELL, FRENCH COVER VERSIONS ANYWAY...

LE JOUR ET LA NUIT

IN FACT, 'ALL DAY AND ALL OF THE NIGHT' BECAME 'LE JOUR ET LA NUIT' BY LES LIONCEAUX!

THE FAMOUS DICK RIVERS GOT IN ON IT!

LA CHEULE QUI ME PLAÎT *

* "YOU REALLY GOT ME"

HE EVEN GOT INTO A FIGHT WITH FRANK ALAMO ABOUT 'TIRED OF WAITING FOR YOU,' WHICH BECAME...

SO KINKS SONGS WERE ADAPTED BY FRENCH SINGERS AND SONGWRITERS WHO THEN MADE SOME GOOD MONEY OFF OF ROYALTIES...

MA VIE A T'ATTENHENDRE

3

AND THE LIST GOES ON. MICHÈLE TORR EVEN DID A COVER OF 'DANDY'

DANDY! ♪ DANDY!

AND DANIEL GUICHARD JUST HAD TO DO A VERSION OF THE SADDEST KINKS SONG, 'DEATH OF A CLOWN'...

LAISSE TES JOURNAUX

A RECORD HE COULD ONLY BEAT FOR SHEER SADNESS A FEW YEARS LATER WITH HIS OWN SONG, 'MON VIEUX'! HIS SHREDDED OVERCOAT SENT KLEENEX SALES THROUGH THE ROOF.

'A WELL RESPECTED MAN', ONE OF THEIR BEST-WRITTEN SONGS, WAS COVERED BY MARC LAFERRIÈRE... AND IT WAS JUST AN INTSTRUMENTAL VERSION! LISTEN TO A FEW BARS OF THE TRUMPET.

COIN COIN COIN ♪

THERE IT IS...

AND FINALLY, THE BEST OF ALL, SERGE LAMA TRANSFORMED 'APEMAN' INTO 'SUPERMAN,' WHICH WAS A HUGE SUCCESS.

DITES POURQUOI JE PASSE AUPRÈS DES FEMMES POUM POUM... POUR SUPERMAAN ?

THEN, AFTER THAT, THERE WAS A SHORT LULL, BUT FRANCE CAME TO APPRECIATE 'YOU REALLY GOT ME' AGAIN IN THE LATE 1970S — WITH THE VAN HALEN VERSION.

TOU POU DOU DOUM

AT THE SAME TIME, IT WASN'T THEIR BEST SONG...

DUTCH PEOPLE DO IT WELL...

Her death in October 1970, at the age of 27—a little more than a year after the death of the Rolling Stones' fallen angel Brian Jones, and a month after the death of Jimi Hendrix—made Janis Joplin one of the first martyrs of rock and roll. As it did for other departed rock stars, her death made her a symbol: a symbol of the end of the carefree exuberance of the sixties and their utopias; a symbol of the failure of the hippie revolution in California, crushed by the system, as were its messengers. While Janis Joplin's passing traumatized the flower generation, above all it pointed to the tragedy of the artist herself; it was the epilogue of a short journey, a destiny as grandiose as it was moving—the accelerated rock version of Billie Holiday. After leaving her native Texas, Joplin found a family among the hippie community of San Francisco, which was more supportive of her hedonistic and spiritual aspirations. With her first group Big Brother and the Holding Company—the psychedelic blues band that was her starting point and that put her in the spotlight—she performed in the momentous and iconic music festivals at Monterey and Woodstock.

She also simultaneously became a key figure in the budding and anti-establishment Summer of Love in 1967. An independent woman with many men and a loud mouth, she subverted the clichés of the male rock star. Less than four years later, though, the icon was left lonely and disillusioned, and became a bitter, alcoholic caricature of what she had been. With so many questions about the value of life—a life that inspired the movie The Rose (with Bette Middler in the leading role)—she grew world-weary and withered. One statement says everything about her confusion: "On stage, I make love to 25,000 different people. Then I go home alone."

Two months before succumbing to an overdose of pure heroin, Janis Joplin raised money for a proper gravestone for the legendary Bessie Smith, the blues singer who had died thirty years earlier. It was a way of giving her due to one of the voices that had left an indelible mark on her. Like other female singers (Karen Dalton or, more recently, Amy Winehouse), Joplin had white skin, but the vocal chords and soul of a 'black mama' twice her age. Inside her frail body there was an exceptional performer, capable of taking other people's songs to a new level, rivaling Aretha Franklin or Otis Redding. The artist with whom Janis had the most in common (alcohol, excess, drunken poetry), however, was Jim Morrison, the capricious singer of the Doors, whose lifestyle was just as chaotic as hers. Although they were similar, they never had a chance to become the perfect beatnik couple. Joplin, whose main pastime was getting laid (as Catel and Philippe Paringaux's authentic story suggests), seemed to have been attracted to Jim.

SELECTED DISCOGRAPHY

Cheap Thrills (with Big Brother and the Holding Company, 1968)
The first Big Brother album didn't highlight Joplin's mind-blowing talents clearly enough—a mistake that was corrected on this second album, on which her voice erupts like a soulful fountain.

Pearl (1971)
Released posthumously (Joplin died while it was being recorded), this final solo album—coming after the disappointing I Got Dem Ol' Kozmic Blues Again Mama!—remains one of the most beautiful swan songs there is.

But he introduced himself so violently one night that she broke a bottle of whiskey over his head, ending all hopes of a hook-up. The comic artist Robert Crumb had more luck when he was spearheading underground comics in 1968 and was asked to create the album cover for Cheap Thrills, the second album released by Big Brother and the Holding Company. As compensation for his drawing, which immediately entered the pantheon of rock art, he asked to pinch one of her breasts, a request Joplin is said to have accepted at a party. The image we keep of her comes from another cover: her smiling portrait forever captured on Pearl, a posthumous album.

JANIS JOPLIN

1943 — **1970**

A story by
Catel
&
Philippe
Paringaux

From 1967 to 1968:
Big Brother and
the Holding Company
After 1969 :
Janis Joplin

HER DEATH IN
OCTOBER 1970, AT 27,
MADE JANIS JOPLIN
ONE OF THE FIRST
MARTYRS OF
ROCK AND ROLL

PLAYLIST
1 Bye Bye Baby (1967)
2 Intruder (1967)
3 Down on Me (1967)
4 The Last Time (1967)
5 Combination of the Two (1968)
6 Summertime (1968)
7 Piece of my Heart (1968)
8 Turtle Blues (1968)
9 Ball and Chain (1968)
10 Try (Just a Little Bit Harder) (1969)
11 Kozmic Blues (1969)
12 Little Girl Blue (1969)
13 Move Over (1971)
14 A Woman Left Lonely (1971)
15 Cry Baby (1971)
16 Me & Bobby McGee (1971)
17 Mercedes Benz (1971)
18 Trust Me (1971)
19 Get it While You Can (1971)
20 Tell Mama (1971)

FRENCH KISS

April 14, 1969...

Modest, discreet in appearance, but really prouder than a peacock if he's recognized by a few fans, a rock critic— still a novice, but arrogant—enters the music sanctuary.

Mister Paringaux from ROCK&FOLK? Here's your ticket!

Thanks to the monopoly of the press, the fans are reduced to taking everything this self-proclaimed Messiah prophesizes as the Word in their monthly musical bible of electric miracles.

Cool, huh? This same guy emptied his pockets so he could see the Beatles from the very last row. Now he's got a box seat reserved. A real prince.

From his plush crimson nest, he can see and be seen.

The theater slowly fills. So slowly, in fact, that it doesn't fill up. From up on high, filled with young pride, he looks over the hundreds of empty seats with indignation.

JANIS JOPLIN !

clap! clap! clap!

Could it be that no one in the depths of France has read his review of Cheap Thrills?

One advantage was that it made him feel like the CHOSEN one.

TRRYYY♪♫ TRRRYYY

a little bit ♫ harder

And finally... **her.** Crossing the stage as if she wanted to break it with her heels. Clearly distraught to see her vocal acrobatics would fall upon an ocean of empty seats.

Especially since right next to him, floating in a cloud of patchouli, shooting stars named Patti or Maria were giggling while their slender arms chimed with the requisite bangles.

And what's the thinking behind trying to capitalize on the success of a group of stoned amateurs by setting out on tour with pros who are otherwise less... cosmic? Business is business, ok.

Her **voice** hasn't changed. But still...

Seeming at once absent and furious, she falls into a routine, just like you'd carry out a chore.

And then the diva's high-notes die along with the thin applause.

He should have known. He's handsome and he's dumb, so why did he decide to enter this volcanic woman's dressing room right after that fiasco of a gig?

Her eyes were so dark behind the veil of her hair that he immediately recognized his mistake.

With every step he took toward her, he couldn't help but think of the nickname her classmates had given her in Texas: "The ugliest man on campus."

Did she want to give him a little piece of her heart? Hmm...

Come on...

She kissed him for a long time. Voraciously. A French kiss, Janis style. Her breath reeked of alcohol and other things too, a smell of perfume, sweat, and rancid sex emanated from her body.

He almost vomited in her mouth, a real rock-and-roll fairytale.

NOW, FUCK OFF!

The nails that had dug into his flesh released themselves and she pushed him away in fury. Once more she yelled the last three words he would ever hear her say (except on vinyl).

Then he waited 489 days for the frog to turn into a princess and agree to marry him...

But the story is well known: she didn't wait for him. At Woodstock singing "Bobby McGee," she gave herself all the love in the world and the Mercedes Benz to go with it.

Then one night in October 1970, his princess of one night pricked herself with a needle before falling into a sleep so deep it was eternal. And he began to wonder if he really was the Prince Charming he thought he was back then...

Let's first dispel a myth: the name Pink Floyd has nothing to do with pink flamingos. In 1965, to name the group formed by Nick Mason (drums), Richard Wright (keyboards), and Roger Waters (bass), lead singer Syd Barrett combined the names of two American blues singers—Pink Anderson and Floyd Council—and created the Pink Floyd Sound. At the time, rhythm and blues from the United States was what fueled these young English rockers: their song list included standards by Chuck Berry and Bo Diddley. Gradually, Pink Floyd was drawn to the avant-garde, with Barrett's compositions lending themselves more and more to instrumental improvisation. In 1967, the group was at the center of London's underground scene: each concert was a happening and their favorite club was the UFO ("Unidentified Flying Object" or "Underground Freak Out").

A story by Li-An

PINK FLOYD

1964 – 2005

When David Gilmour came to stand in for Syd Barret, who was thrown out of the band because of his schizophrenic behavior, Pink Floyd began exploiting the newest technology (keyboards, drum machines) with the goal of creating soaring and illusory soundscapes. Their instrumental passages began to overtake the usual structures of pop music.

In 1973 the group impressed the world with its adventurous (but also pretentious) *Dark Side of the Moon*, especially with the song "Money," which featured the rhythmic sounds of closing cash registers. In the United States, the success of *Dark Side* was incredible: it remained on

THE POPULARITY OF THIS ENGLISH BAND'S SOARING MUSIC STEMMED FROM ITS EVOCATIVE POWER

Billboard's top 100 for more than 700 weeks! Then Roger Waters, who was already writing lyrics, became the main songwriter, making the songs much more personal. Not only does the grandiloquent rock opera *The Wall* recount the erring ways of a fictitious rock star (named Pink), but it also unravels Waters' own Freudian knots. After the tremendous success of the hit 'Another Brick in the Wall, Part 2,' there developed a war of egos in the 1980s. Roger Waters left Pink Floyd, but this certainly didn't rattle the band's success. Up until the time the band broke up in the mid-1990s, Pink Floyd survived on its moneymakers, keeping their young fans' flames alive through albums and halfhearted tours. The ultimate overhaul took place during a fundraising concert in 2005. The death of the keyboardist Richard Wright, after Barrett's, made other such forays impossible.

Although the faces of the band members always meant little—they're English gentlemen and poor candidates for stardom—the work of Pink Floyd immediately conjures up visions. When their music wasn't being used for soundtracks in Barbet Schroeder's movies (*More*, *La Vallée*) or Michelangelo Antonioni's *Zabriskie Point*, it was accompanied by powerful images. For example, there were live concerts with psychedelic slide projections. There are so many images: from the *Atom Heart Mother* cow, to the empty Pompeii amphitheater; from the pyramid on *The Dark Side of the Moon*, to the chimneys of the Battersea Power Station and the inflatable pig Algie on *Animals*; from the wall on *The Wall* made from three hundred cardboard bricks, to the blinking LED on the case of *Pulse*, the last live double CD . . . Each has helped reinforce the strange imagery of a band that was the first multimedia pop act, long before Gorillaz or Daft Punk. In terms of exaggeration and visual excess, Pink Floyd almost outdid Jean-Michel Jarre, even if it meant slipping into the grotesque (the unrealized project to make an inflatable pyramid, for example). In the six pages that follow, presented as a treasure hunt, the comic artist Li-An pays tribute to the songs on *Meddle* and draws on the group's symbols: the cow from *Atom Heart Mother* quotes *The Wall*; the pyramid from *The Dark Side of the Moon* rises from nothingness; and musicians straight out of a Western perform "Wish You Were Here." The popularity of this English band's soaring music stemmed from its evocative power and, several decades later, influenced some of the sophisticated work by Sébastien Tellier, Air, Radiohead, Archive, and the Mars Volta.

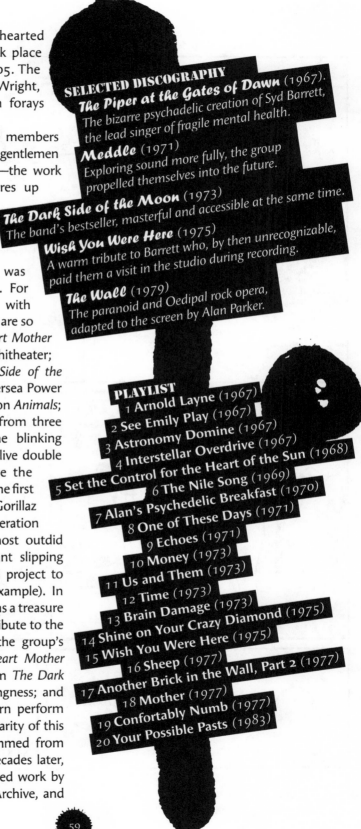

SELECTED DISCOGRAPHY

The Piper at the Gates of Dawn (1967).
The bizarre psychedelic creation of Syd Barrett, the lead singer of fragile mental health.

Meddle (1971)
Exploring sound more fully, the group propelled themselves into the future.

The Dark Side of the Moon (1973)
The band's bestseller, masterful and accessible at the same time.

Wish You Were Here (1975)
A warm tribute to Barrett who, by then unrecognizable, paid them a visit in the studio during recording.

The Wall (1979)
The paranoid and Oedipal rock opera, adapted to the screen by Alan Parker.

PLAYLIST

1 Arnold Layne (1967)
2 See Emily Play (1967)
3 Astronomy Domine (1967)
4 Interstellar Overdrive (1967)
5 Set the Control for the Heart of the Sun (1968)
6 The Nile Song (1969)
7 Alan's Psychedelic Breakfast (1970)
8 One of These Days (1971)
9 Echoes (1971)
10 Money (1973)
11 Us and Them (1973)
12 Time (1973)
13 Brain Damage (1973)
14 Shine on Your Crazy Diamond (1975)
15 Wish You Were Here (1975)
16 Sheep (1977)
17 Another Brick in the Wall, Part 2 (1977)
18 Mother (1977)
19 Confortably Numb (1977)
20 Your Possible Pasts (1983)

LOOK, MOM! THERE IS A PLANE IN THE SKY!

WELCOME MY SON.

WELCOME TO THE MACHINE...

shine on you crazy diamond...

SELECTED DISCOGRAPHY

1967: The Jimi Hendrix Experience
From 1968: Jimi Hendrix

Are You Experienced (1967)

For this incredible experiment, Hendrix, leading his trio (Mitch Mitchell on drums, Noel Redding on bass), concocted his own psychadelic blues.

Axis: Bold as Love (1967)

On a roll and playing with stereo effects for the first time, the guitarist ended 1967 with a thing of beauty.

Electric Ladyland (1968)

Incessantly experimenting as if he were an entire band himself, Hendrix tore apart the pop format.

Band of Gypsies (1970)

With Buddy Miles on drums and Billy Cox on bass, this live sweat-fest shows Hendrix's funkiest side.

Did he know he was doomed? On his first album, barely three years before his death, a song warned: "Will I live tomorrow?/Well, I just can't say/But I know for sure/I don't live today." The following year, Hendrix was just as explicit in "Voodoo Child," a legendary song from his personal statement *Electric Ladyland*, announcing: "If I don't meet you no more in this world then uh/I'll meet you on the next one/But don't be late." During his spectacular four-year journey of surging creativity, Jimi Hendrix inspired the opinion—surely something from off the top of his curled head—that he was a kind of extraterrestrial visitor passing through our world. But we can also dream and believe that when he disappeared from our reality, he entered another spatial and temporal plane, where he's now once again revolutionizing rock and roll and the vocabulary of his favorite instrument, the guitar, with effect pedals. François Ayroles, in the pages that follow, seems to think so! In any case, the American singer left us enough material to dive into and still celebrate decades after his death. His discography, which in his lifetime consisted of three albums (one, a double) and one live album (*Band of Gypsies*), would take on another dimension after his death.

A number of near-complete collections of his work now present all the studio recordings made during his last two years. Some were meant for a new dawn, for *First Rays of the New Rising Sun*, a sequel to *Electric Ladyland*.

HENDRIX LEFT US ENOUGH MATERIAL TO DIVE INTO AND STILL CELEBRATE DECADES AFTER HIS DEATH

An unwilling member of the "27 club"—that unofficial and posthumous group of musicians who died before their 28th birthdays (including Janis Joplin, Jim Morrison, Brian Jones, and, from another generation, but also from Seattle, Kurt Cobain)—Hendrix, who died from taking a massive overdose of sleeping pills on September 17, 1970, continues to excite our imaginations. Some people who lived through that time have facetiously suggested that Hendrix, who, between 1961 and 1966, played an unremarkable bit part behind the Isley Brothers, Little Richard, and Sam Cooke, must have made a Faustian deal at a crossroads to have suddenly become a molten guitarist on his way to London in 1966. This is a fairy tale reminiscent of the legend surrounding the bluesman Robert Johnson. Johnson was said to have met the devil at a crossroads and to have sold his soul in exchange for superhuman talent, one that enabled him to write (between

PLAYLIST
1 Hey Joe (1966)
2 Purple Haze (1967)
3 Manic Depression (1967)
4 The Wind Cries Mary (1967)
5 Fire (1967)
6 Foxy Lady (1967)
7 Red House (1967)
8 Wait Until Tomorrow (1967)
9 Little Wing (1967)
10 If 6 was 9 (1967)
11 Castles Made of Sand (1967)
12 Bold as Love (1967)
13 Crosstown Traffic (1968)
14 Gypsy Eyes (1968)
15 Burning of the Midnight Lamp (1968)
16 All Along the Watchtower (1968)
17 Voodoo Child (Sligh Return) (1968)
18 Machine Gun (1969)
19 Angel (1970)
20 Ezy Rider (1970)

A story by François Ayroles

JiMi HENDRiX

1942 – 1970

1936 and 1937) classic blues songs that later propelled the careers of the Rolling Stones and Led Zeppelin. At once a colorful pop star and a spokesperson for hippie youth, Hendrix (and his destiny) was considerably more public than Johnson. He would participate in all the "flower power" gatherings, starting with the Summer of Love in 1967, performing at the Monterey Pop Festival (June), Woodstock (August 1969), and at the third Isle of Wight Festival a few weeks before his death (in August 1970). He protested against the war in Vietnam when he used his guitar as a sound gun for the song "Machine Gun," and when he revised the national anthem, the "Star Spangled Banner," at Woodstock. Nearly four decades after his passing, his legacy is not so much political as it is musical, influencing everyone from Prince to the Roots, Iggy Pop, and the Red Hot Chili Peppers, and even jazz (Miles Davis has forever recruited successors) and heavy metal guitar heroes.

The news had spread fast, and he immediately identified its owner...

...and realized the profit that could be made.

miles & Jimi

We ended up finding the arm at a fan club, where it was worshipped like a relic.

It must have gotten into the hands of a good embalmer. It's in such good condition after all these years.

They didn't find a ring or bracelet.

SCRITCH

We'll let you go, your guests are waiting for you.

72

Don Van Vliet, the fantastic brain behind Captain Beefheart, left the music world in 1982, after wreaking true havoc for two decades. He used colors to describe ideas, considered Vincent Van Gogh to be his ultimate hero, once took his musicians to a Salvador Dalí exhibition to inspire them, and ultimately realized his dream. He became a painter with a comfortable career. Often abstract and always multicolored, his work is an extension of his singular musical language, a kind of dialect combining the rough diction of the blues and the wild energy of free jazz. According to the praise of the cult rock critic Lester Bangs, who was always attracted to innovation on the fringe, Van Vliet created his own vocabulary, one that was both avant-garde and primitive, the result of impromptu combinations and disjointed inspirations. Captain Beefheart, a name used by Frank Zappa (Van Vliet's friend and another offbeat rocker) in a film script that was never realized, was born in hippie California, but never subscribed to the flower power philosophy. With the voice (ranging several octaves) of a preacher gone astray, influenced by the scratchy and powerful sound of Howlin' Wolf, Von Vliet and his Magic Band were first a blues band, covering the Stones and Bo Diddley. But good form soon fell by the wayside and became a thing of the past. Ry Cooder, then a young guitar prodigy, wouldn't stay with the group for long, remarking justifiably that "it wasn't really the blues." In his defense, the fact that Van Vliet once ran away mid-concert—he later claimed that he had seen a fan turn into a fish and a bubble come out of its mouth—may have turned him off.

Like Zappa, Don Van Vliet was an odd bandleader, at once a tyrant and a guru. While recording the legendary Trout Mask Replica, it's said that his musicians were practically sequestered and somewhat brainwashed . . . not to mention the sessions that lasted two full days

CAPTAIN

DON VAN VLIET, THE FANTASTIC BRAIN BEHIND CAPTAIN BEEFHEART, LEFT THE MUSIC WORLD IN 1982, AFTER WREAKING TRUE HAVOC FOR TWO DECADES

and the money that was obviously missing. But the sacrifices that Van Vliet demanded weren't gratuitous. A unique skipper, the Captain had a firm grip on the rudder and saw uncharted territory ahead. But he alone knew how to land there. Self-taught—he played the saxophone without knowing the notes—he knew how to surround himself with the people who could help him get to where he wanted. The musicians that accompanied him during his peak years

SELECTED DISCOGRAPHY

Safe as Milk (1967)
The Captain, with Ry Cooder on guitar, plays his part in the blues revival, although there is some indication of the delirium to come.

Trout Mask Replica (1969)
Produced by Zappa, complete madness and pure beauty combined.

Shiny Beast (1978)
New life for Van Vliet's Dada blues.

A story by Jean-Michel Thiriet

1966 – 1982

BEEFHEART

(the drummer John "Drumbo" French, the guitarist Zoot Horn Rollo, Jeff Cotton, etc.) were such masters of their instruments that they gave the impression of improvising what was, in fact, premeditated and disciplined. Matt Groening, the future creator of *The Simpsons*, says that at the age of fifteen, before falling under Beefheart's spell, he was disconcerted by what seemed to be a random performance.

It comes as no surprise that this fiercely anti-commercial music was never popular—the rare attempts to make Beefheart trendy in the 1970s remain cynical failures—but it helped liberate countless artists who would later be influenced by his approach. Some even followed in his steps. After his wife made him discover Van Vliet, the rock growler Tom Waits is said to have had

an epiphany that directly influenced his later albums, which became less cramped, more in the vein of jazz. Because he rejected norms and smooth forms, when he came back to music in 1978 (*Shiny Beast*), Captain Beefheart was celebrated by certain musicians from the post-punk scene (including John Lydon, formerly of the Sex Pistols) as a distant relative, but one that decisively helped open their minds. John Peel, the legendary English radio DJ from the BBC, took it one step further. Over several decades he introduced many artists—including PJ Harvey, Joy Division, and David Bowie—when they were just starting out. He says that if he were to name one genius of pop music, it would be Beefheart. As you'll see, Thiriet agrees.

CAPTAIN BEEFHEART

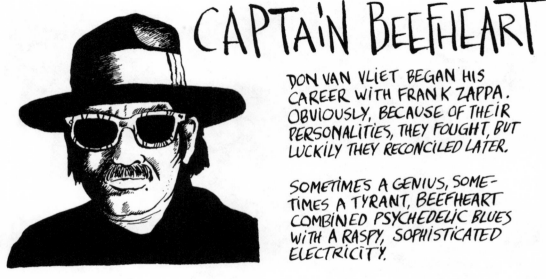

DON VAN VLIET BEGAN HIS CAREER WITH FRANK ZAPPA. OBVIOUSLY, BECAUSE OF THEIR PERSONALITIES, THEY FOUGHT, BUT LUCKILY THEY RECONCILED LATER.

SOMETIMES A GENIUS, SOMETIMES A TYRANT, BEEFHEART COMBINED PSYCHEDELIC BLUES WITH A RASPY, SOPHISTICATED ELECTRICITY.

IN JANUARY 1968, BEEFHEART AND HIS MAGIC BAND PLAYED ON THE BEACHES OF CANNES !! SOMEONE WHO HARDLY EVER PLAYED IN EUROPE CAME TO PLAY ON THE BEACHES OF CANNES!!

TCR 01: 02: 31: 17

IT'S STRANGE TO SEE BEEFHEART IN FRONT OF LE MARTINEZ, WHERE WE'RE MORE USED TO SEEING BLAND MOVIE STARS...
IN 1968, I WAS TEN YEARS OLD. I COULD HAVE BEEN THE PHOTOGRAPHER YOU SEE ABOVE...
EXCEPT THAT IN 1968, I WAS DISCOVERING THE BEATLES...
IN ALL LIKELIHOOD, I WOULD HAVE FOUND IT TOO NOISY AND CHAOTIC. STUPID IDIOT.

EWWW

ON 11.22.80, BEEFHEART WAS ON *SATURDAY NIGHT LIVE.* HE PLAYED TWO SONGS IN FRONT OF A SOMEWHAT UPTIGHT TELEVISION AUDIENCE... IT WAS A REMARKABLE SHOW WITH ERIC DREW FELDMAN ON THE KEYBOARD AND BASS GUITAR. HE WOULD ALSO GO ON TO PLAY WITH FRANK BLACK, PJ HARVEY, AND SNAKE FINGER. THERE'S SOMEONE WHO KNOWS HOW TO CHOOSE HIS PARTNERS!

A FREE SOPRANO SAX SOLO, QUITE VIOLENT AND DISSONANT. IT WAS OVERWHELMING. AT THE END, RIGHT BEFORE THE APPLAUSE, SOMEONE IN THE AUDIENCE SCREAMED "*BULLSHIT!!*" BUT WHO WAS THE VILE BLASPHEMER? HOW DARE HE, THAT HEATHEN!? LET'S ISSUE A FATWA!!

THAT SIMPLETON WAS IN FACT RADAMES PERA, THE ACTOR IN *LITTLE HOUSE ON THE PRAIRIE* AND *KUNG FU!* HAHAHA! I DEVISED A NICE LITTLE TORTURE MACHINE JUST FOR HIM...

...BUT IN READING ABOUT THE CONCERT, I LEARNED THAT HE LATER BECAME FRIENDS WITH THE MUSICIANS. AND AT THE NEXT SHOW, HE COMPLAINED WHEN IT WAS CUT SHORT. HE COULD HAVE WORKED THAT OUT A LITTLE SOONER. STUPID IDIOT.

SOURCES : BEEFHEART.COM

THIRIET

Andy Warhol's conceptuality, Japanese Kabuki theater, and the ways of New York transvestites; the attitude of the New York Dolls, the songs of the Beatles, the Stones, and Lou Reed, and the experimentation of Kraftwerk, the German techno pioneers; Philadelphia soul and disco, Orwell's prophetic *1984*, the Droggies in Stanley Kubrick's *Clockwork Orange*; the movements of the mime Marcel Marceau, William Burroughs' cut-up literary technique . . . All these things at some point fed David Bowie's creativity. Never petty as an artist, he always returned the favor to those who inspired him, helping Mott the Hoople, the veterans of glam rock, and Lou Reed to attain the success their influence deserved (it was thanks to Bowie that Reed, formerly of the Velvet Underground, hit gold with *Transformer* and "Walk on the Wild Side"). Then, from 1972–1973, Iggy Pop and his Stooges survived on the generosity of Mainman, the company founded by Tony De Fries (Bowie's legendary manager) that showered them with privileges and financed their indulgences.

The first entirely postmodern rocker, at once a chameleon and a vampire, David Bowie has always foreseen trends and anticipated shifts in music and fashion. His sense of timing is impressive, almost innate: his first hit "Space Oddity" happily coincided with the landing of the Apollo spacecraft on the moon. He then immediately stepped out of his hippie garb and into the flamboyant threads of Ziggy Stardust, the androgynous glam-rock hero, inspired as much by Marc Bolan of T. Rex as by Gene Vincent (with his shattered leg) and the play *Pork*, written by Andy Warhol. Already a pop star by then, Bowie opened minds by revealing his bisexuality to the media, backing up his declaration with suggestive poses during concerts—on his knees, he would take Mick Ronson's guitar strings into his mouth. During a concert in London in July 1973, he staged Ziggy's suicide—a surprise to all—and set about introducing a series of personas that would embody the future mutations of his music. His incredible body of work (a dozen essential albums at the very least) is thanks in part to this ability to close chapters, even if it means killing off his own characters and reinventing himself as someone better.

This love of changing identity explains the radical shifts that culminated in the 1990s. During the 1980s he was very much in the spotlight because of the success of *Let's Dance*. But he began the following decade in near-anonymity, joining Tin Machine, a group he founded with friends in order to dive back into the joys of the rawest kind of rock. Predictably, Tin Machine failed. Afterward, and certainly as a reaction to the experience, he intertwined

DAVID

his voice with the electronic textures of techno and jungle music. For *Outside* (1995), recorded with Brian Eno (a musician who brought the avant-garde into pop with Roxy Music and Talking Heads), he split into many characters, epitomizing artistic schizophrenia. But Bowie (born David Jones) was not only an incredible synthesis: behind his intelligence and flair there lies one of the most moving singers and brilliant songwriters—a perfect chameleon. The proof: Bowie's songs have as much life as he does. They form a repertoire that is vast and expansive enough to transcend eras and trends. Nirvana (a few months before Kurt Cobain's death), Nine Inch Nails, New Wave bands like the Cure or Blondie, contemporary composers like Philip Glass, the Brazilian Seu Jorge, the hard-rockers of Van Halen, and some of the explorers of electronica—all have covered songs by Bowie. So even though this blond with mismatched eyes built up his art by picking the brains of others, his legacy has proven more crucial than what he borrowed to begin with.

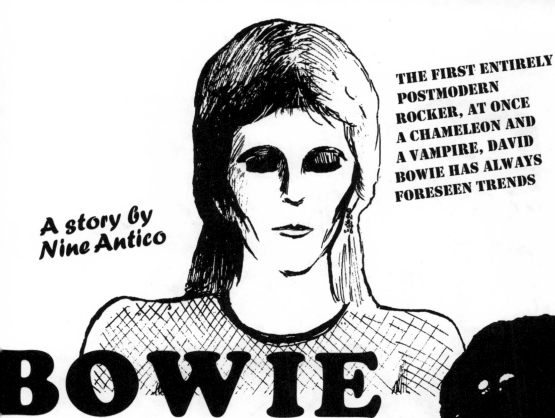

THE FIRST ENTIRELY POSTMODERN ROCKER, AT ONCE A CHAMELEON AND A VAMPIRE, DAVID BOWIE HAS ALWAYS FORESEEN TRENDS

A story by Nine Antico

BOWIE

BORN IN 1947

SELECTED DISCOGRAPHY

Hunky Dory (1971)
Only classics on this album. Bowie without the makeup.

Ziggy Stardust (1972)
The life and death of Ziggy, the extraterrestrial rock star. The height of glam rock.

Station to Station (1976)
Icy and sophisticated, an album full of fascinating and complex songs.

Heroes (1977)
The high point, between Low and Lodger, of the trilogy Bowie recorded with Brian Eno about Berlin.

Scary Monsters (1980)
The last pure masterpiece before the hits of Let's Dance.

PLAYLIST

1 Space Oddity (1969)
2 The Man Who Sold the World (1970)
3 Changes (1971)
4 Life on Mars (1971)
5 Ziggy Stardust (1972)
6 Moonage Daydream (1972)
7 Aladdin Sane (1973)
8 Sweet Thing (1974)
9 Young Americans (1975)
10 Golden Years (1976)
11 TVC15 (1976)
12 Sound and Vision (1977)
13 Heroes (1977)
14 Look Back in Anger (1978)
15 Ashes to Ashes (1980)
16 Modern Love (1983)
17 Let's Dance (1983)
18 Jump they Say (1993)
19 I'm Deranged (1995)
20 I'm Afraid of Americans (1997)

*TONY DE FRIES CREATED THE MANAGEMENT COMPANY "MAINMAN" AND HIRED FRIENDS OF ANDY WARHOL TO WORK WITH DAVID BOWIE (TONY ZANETTA, WAYNE COUNTY, LEEE BLACK CHILDERS, CHERRY VANILLA, JAMIE DE CARLO).

OH, BUT IT'S SAD...

HIS SMALL, STRANGE EYES ARE CLOSED...

AND THIS PRETTY AQUILINE NOSE!

WHAT A STRANGE FACE...

IT'S TOO BAD, HUH?

AND I WAS COUNTING ON HIM TO TURN ME INTO A STAR!

WHOA! WHY'S HE LYING DOWN LIKE THAT, HE LOOKS DEAD!

BABE! WHERE HAVE YOU BEEN? DID YOU SPEND THE CONCERT IN THE BATHROOM AGAIN?

ZIGGY IS OVER, HONEY!

BUT... WHEN I LEFT, EVERYTHING WAS FINE, HE WAS SCRATCHING THE GUITAR WITH HIS TEETH... HE WAS SO SEXY!

THEY'RE THE ONES WE SHOULD FEEL SORRY FOR! LOOK AT THEM! THEY LOOK COMPLETELY LOST...

ANDY, YOU THINK THEY'RE GOING TO THROW ALL THAT MAKEUP AWAY?

If Charles Berberian hadn't been so adamant—he chose him over a much more indisputable giant—Elton John surely wouldn't be in this book. As he explains in these pages, our opinion of the bespectacled singer is, in fact, based on the image he has been promoting for two decades. After several hits in the 1980s that ring like jingles, the Englishman seemed to have turned in his famous eccentricity and extravagant wardrobe for extremely bad taste (posing with his poodle), becoming a caricature worthy of *La Cage aux Folles*. We also associate John with the sad memory of 'Candle in the Wind,' the tearful syrup he poured on at the funeral of Diana, Princess of Wales, in 1997. But we forget that that song, written with the English lyricist Bernie Taupin in 1973, was originally dedicated to Marilyn Monroe. In the same way, although John has been collaborating on sterile Disney productions since *The Lion King* in 2000, one of his old songs illuminated one of the definitive movies about rock and roll. A tender tribute to a groupie, 'Tiny Dancer' (1971) gives prominence to one of the most moving moments in *Almost Famous*, the feature-length film inspired by the experience of director Cameron Crow as a teenage journalist at the magazine *Rolling Stone*. John also appears in Ken Russell's screen adaptation of the rock opera *Tommy* (1975), next to the members of The Who (who made the movie), Eric Clapton, and Tina Turner. He can also claim to be the reason behind John Lennon's last concert in 1974: Lennon had promised to join him on stage if the new version they recorded of "Lucy in the Sky with Diamonds" made the charts. As for "Your Song," the tune that truly launched Elton John's career, Lennon had previously stated that he considered it to be the best thing to have happened in music since . . . well, the Beatles. And as far as Paul McCartney's concerned: there's a crazy legend, devised from songs played

SELECTED DISCOGRAPHY

Elton John (1970)
His second album. Good songs with classy arrangements by Paul Buckmaster.

Tumbleweed Connection (1971)
A very successful concept album, the American way.

Madman Across the Water (1971)
Bernie Taupin supremely inspired, Elton a nimble as can be, and, as always, the brilliance of Buckmaster.

Goodbye Yellow Brickroad (1973)
A double album, at times a bit heavy, but very fulfilling.

PLAYLIST

1 Empty Sky (1969)
2 Your Song (1970)
3 Take Me to the Pilot (1970)
4 Son of Your Father (1970)
5 My Father's Gun (1970)
6 Tiny Dancer (1971)
7 Levon (1971)
8 Madman Across the Water (1971)
9 Honky Cat (1972)
10 Rocket Man (I Think It's Going to Be a Long, Long Time) (1972)
11 Mona Lisas and Mad Hatters (1972)
12 Daniel (1972)
13 Crocodile Rock (1972)
14 Candle in the Wind (1973)
15 Bennie and the Jets (1973)
16 Goodbye Yellow Brick Road (1973)
17 Saturday Night's Alright for Fighting (1973)
18 Don't Let the Sun Go Down on Me (1974)
19 Pinball Wizard (1974)
20 Captain Fantastic and the Brown Dirt Cowboy (1975)

Elton John

BORN IN 1947

backward and from supposed signs, that says he was replaced in the late 1960s by a twin. Similarly, there are two Elton Johns. Especially since his voice lost its charm after a throat operation in 1986 that took away his falsetto.

In the early 1970s, the man who had not yet changed his official

A story by Charles Berberian

PLING PLONG PLUNG

TAP TAP

name (Reginald Kenneth Dwight) to Elton Hercules John was a successful pop star partly because his band was a kind of "dream team" of English rock. A child piano prodigy—Dwight played his scales both at the Royal Academy of Music and in a pub—he joined Bluesology, a group that accompanied American rhythm and blues idols (the Isley Brothers, Major Lance). He walked away with experience and a new name, which he formed from the names of the band's saxophonist (Elton Dean, who later created Soft Machine with Robert Wyatt) and its lead singer (Long John Baldry).

IN THE EARLY 1970S, ELTON HERCULES JOHN WAS A SUCCESSFUL POP STAR PARTLY BECAUSE HIS BAND WAS A KIND OF "DREAM TEAM" OF ENGLISH ROCK

After answering an ad for talent, he began working with Bernie Taupin, first by correspondence. "I never understood his lyrics," John once said mischievously—he knows how much he owes to Taupin's humor and poetry. During his most prolific and creative period, John also benefited from an amazing group behind him that was almost glam (Davey Johnstone on guitar, Nigel Olsson on drums, and Dee Murray on bass), but also from Paul Buckmaster, the cellist and arranger on Bowie's *Space Oddity*, and on Miles Davis' *On the Corner*. This is the Elton John that Charles Berberian cherishes; not the one behind "Nikita" or "Don't Go Breaking My Heart."

ELTON John

PLING

PLONG

Since 1975, Elton John hasn't recorded a single good album. But before that, it's hard to find a single fault in his discography. (Ok, maybe one or two weak songs in the ten albums recorded over five years).

Elton John and his group in the 1970s

But the people who admired him at the beginning of his career are the first to send him straight to syrupy-serenade hell.

Elton with lots of new hair.

Elton and his lyricist, Bernie Taupin.

FOR those who
only know his
most soul-
destroying hits
and his most
Recent wigs,
it's hard to
believe that
Elton could
have ever
written a
decent
melody.

Rocket-Man

Elton on
the Road
to glory

One night, when he was still a Rising Star, Elton played a concert dressed as a gorrilla. He Learned that the Stooges were going to be Performing that same night, in the same town. After his set, without changing, he Rushed out to see Iggy Pop and even tried to join him on the mic.

Elton as a wild animal →

The Stooges flipped out and thought they were being attacked by a real beast...

...and
threw their
instruments
at him.

Elton was
knocked
out.

Doesn't he deserve just a
little attention for this story alone?

Elton always was a bit of a prankster.

PLING PLONG PLUNG

TAP TAP

Charles Berberian

* Listen to the album "Madman Across the Water" first.

A story by Killoffer

SELECTED DISCOGRAPHY

Led Zeppelin I and II (1969)
Although their roots are in blues, this English band invented the hard-rock formula.

Led Zeppelin IV (1971)
Powerful, but more ambitious and mystical. The key album.

Physical Graffiti (1975)
A tremendous, motley double album.

Epic musical flights and songs that last forty minutes onstage, marathon tours making record profits, mountains of drugs and alcohol, thugs, body guards . . . The story of Led Zeppelin has been enormous, titanic—as seen in the pages of Killoffer's story, loosely based on *Moby Dick*, a heroic song with a tremendous drum solo. For more than a decade, during which the group would take over the Beatles and ring in the era of popular rock, its members were the insatiable giants of heavy, feral rock music that would take them to the height of fame before the inevitable decline. "There was so much excess around us that no one knew the limit." At the helm was the charismatic Robert Plant, bare of chest and blond of mane. The band's

journey is like that of a J. R. R. Tolkien character (Plant was a fan) who, after being virtuous and heroic, is corrupted by the power of the ring.

They were explosive together from the start (1969). The first member was Jimmy Page, the studio mercenary for the Kinks and The Who, who, with the Yardbirds, followed in the footsteps of other godly guitar heroes, like Eric Clapton and Jeff Beck. Soon after him came John Paul Jones, bassist and arranger (for Donovan); Robert Plant, an unknown with a high, powerful

LED ZEPPELIN

1969 – 1980

voice; and John "Bonzo" Bonham, a drummer with a mighty beat. But if Led Zeppelin (a name that The Who's crazy drummer came up with) took off, it was also thanks to their manager, Peter Grant. The 1973 movie *The Song Remains the Same*, which captures the group's madness in concert, includes some filler scenes that are funny and informative. You see Plant on a horse heading out to search for the Grail; Page (a fan of the occult) at the top of a snow-capped magical mountain; Jones playing a scarecrow in the fairy tale *Jack and the Beanstalk*; and Bonham drag racing. As for Grant, he's tellingly disguised as a mobster. For the first album, this former wrestler and bouncer received an advance in the incredible amount of $200,000 and was never denied full artistic license. To establish Led Zeppelin's success, he felt they should tour mostly in the United States, a first for a British band. Thanks to his iron fist, Page, Plant, Jones, and Bonham could indulge in mystical delirium and powerful, heavy blues—and all in their private jet named the *Mothership*, on which they even had an organ. While the band laid down the foundations of hard rock, they were still much more open-minded than the groups they inspired. Celtic folklore and Eastern sounds made their way into some of their songs and, in concert, the quartet

delved into impressive improvisations, making each concert unique. Among their feats are the eight minutes of "Stairway to Heaven," a rollercoaster of a song that begins with a quiet acoustic sequence, only to transform into a deafening electric monster. Despite its eccentric structure, this song remains one of the most popular tunes on FM radio.

Backstage, the atmosphere was always extreme. Pushed by Richard Cole, one of Grant's colleagues, Led Zeppelin indulged like barbaric revelers in their every urge. Groupie orgies, sexual perversions (one girl is said to have been graced with the touch of a baby shark, and Bonzo fucked in a bathtub filled with baked beans), hotel rooms destroyed by samurai swords and the requisite, mafia-style beatings . . . These Englishmen lived through the 1970s in a bubble, without impunity. As Cole would confess in hindsight, Led Zep lay down the law. The death of Plant's son in 1977, then of Bonham in 1980, reminded them that they were mortal. After their inevitable breakup, Page and Plant reunited for a project about Eastern music (*No Quarter* in 1994). But Plant refused to get the band back together—except on just one occasion. Even so, Led Zeppelin remain *the* reference for many—Jack White of the White Stripes, for one.

ITS MEMBERS WERE THE INSATIABLE GIANTS OF A HEAVY, FERAL ROCK MUSIC THAT WOULD TAKE THEM TO THE HEIGHT OF FAME BEFORE THE INEVITABLE DECLINE

TRANSLATION

PAGES 96-97
Top, left to right:

Imagine islands full of Led Zep
Comac cars, one for each, that makes 4
It's noisy as hell...
The tango is the devil's dance,
He dances it to cool down.
His wife, his daughters, and his maids
cool down this way too...
Erik Satie, Sports et Divertissements

Nothing but Cadillacs

Bottom, left to right:
Charles Darwin made important observations
in developing his theory about the evolution of
the whale. *Noteworthy.*
Life! Such diversity! Hey there, everybody!
As if it were raining women
The whale, both woman and man

Women? They're all ugly and flat

PAGE 98
Just what we need—notes: It's too much. Just
like for horses. Woman notes, then man notes.
For example: Darwin!
Huh! What?
Um... wait a second.
Yes! Excuse me, Darwin. I just wanted to say
that I don't see what's so shocking about the
idea that a rock-and-roll band might go by the
name "Led Zeppelin"...
Or even "Les Ablettes"!
[ah, yes, but]
I mean, it doesn't bother me!
[no]
From a "lasting" point of view, if you will!
[ok]
It doesn't bother me!

There's also Darloose, which used to mean
something.
So: Darloose?

And horse notes...

If you ask me, getting Led Zeppelin into a
Citroen 2CV... I'm used to having two in front,
and two in back...
Or a Cadillac! That's just as good!

Raging...

Led Zeppelin
Like a whale, soaring,
of lead and feathers.

"I just wasn't made for these times." Nick Drake would have identified with the words of Brian Wilson, the other great melancholic soul who strived nevertheless to produce cheerful music with the Beach Boys. According to those close to him, Drake, the singer and guitarist, would have felt more comfortable in the sixteenth century—as a troubadour in Queen Elizabeth's court—than in the late 1960s, rattled by the electricity of rock. In his own lifetime, he endured more bruising failure than hope or success. His three albums only sold a total of some twenty thousand copies on their initial release. But although he was filled with an old-fashioned romanticism, he didn't focus on the past. Guided by the example of Bob Dylan and other songwriters, he dreamed neither of money nor of becoming a star, but instead wanted to communicate with the youth of his generation, to become a spokesperson and a mirror. It was only decades later, after his death, that his songs would touch millions of listeners (ironically, partly thanks to a car ad).

Nick Drake will always be twenty-six years old, an ethereal phantom who slowly slipped away from the world of the living because his music was not understood. "He rejected the world, he never felt happy," his mother has said. Drake was a beloved member of a tight-knit family, and also an athlete and sought-after friend, but suffered from nothing more than a deep melancholy that made him withdraw, that turned him into a mysterious character, a taciturn person who even confounded those closest to him. "If songs were lines in a conversation, the situation would be fine," he wrote in "Hazey Jane II." Yet he wasn't born autistic or sad, as some later portrayals have attempted to suggest. His first album, *Five Leaves Left*, owes part of its autumnal theme to the warning written at the bottom of a pack of cigarette rolling papers. It was his unsuccessful attempts to achieve recognition that increasingly depressed him. He approached the door to his own magical dream world, and finally passed through one night in November 1974, after an overdose of antidepressants that followed a period of a few weeks at a psychiatric hospital. Two years earlier, he had recorded—alone with his guitar—his final testament, the album

NICK DRAKE WILL ALWAYS BE TWENTY-SIX YEARS OLD, AN ETHEREAL PHANTOM WHO SLOWLY SLIPPED AWAY FROM THE WORLD OF THE LIVING

Pink Moon, which is beautiful and somber, like the sound of a clock striking midnight (the hour when he recorded it, in two sessions). After his death, which was thought to be suicide (although nothing has been proven), his family—and especially his sister, Gabrielle—strove to make his music better known. They distributed a few of his unreleased songs, like "Time of No Reply"—it was not included on the first album because there wasn't enough room—which inspired Vincent Vanoli to describe a dreamy encounter between Drake and an Egyptian princess . . . Another period piece.

Finally, a cult formed around Drake's grave, and around the legacy of his songs. Robert Smith, the soul of the Cure, found the name for his band in one of them; Elton John, Gordon Beck, and the jazz pianist Brad Mehldau covered them. Nearly forty years after their release, as if they had been preserved in a time capsule, his three albums still retain all their power. First and foremost, there's his clear and floating voice. (Robert Kirby, a friend from college who arranged his first album, rightly considered his songs to be poetry.) Then there's his acoustic guitar, which Drake used to play his own complex chords. He had his own technique that combined delta blues chords and the rhythms of ragtime, the forerunner of

jazz. Just as with Georges Brassens (although in a different genre), Drake's deceptive simplicity is hard to imitate. One must therefore turn to the fifty-odd songs that this doomed artist left behind for us.

PLAYLIST

1 Time Has Told Me (1969)
2 River Man (1969)
3 Way to Blue (1969)
4 Day Is Done (1969)
5 Cello Song (1969)
6 The Thoughts of Mary Jane (1969)
7 Fruit Tree (1969)
8 I Was Made to Love Magic (1969)
9 Time of No Reply (1969)
10 Hazey Jane II (1970)
11 At The Chime of a City Clock (1970)
12 One of These Things First (1970)
13 Fly (1970)
14 Northern Sky (1970)
15 Pink Moon (1972)
16 Things behind the Sun (1972)
17 Parasite (1972)
18 From the Morning (1972)
19 Riders on the Wheel (1974)
20 Voices (1974)

SELECTED DISCOGRAPHY

Five Leaves Left (1969)
An inspired recording of acoustic, woodsy folk music.

Bryter Later (1970)
With help from musicians like John Cale, formerly of the Velvet Underground, Drake flirts with jazz and soul.

Pink Moon (1972)
Short but intense, a series of songs performed solo.

Made to Love Magic (2004)
A must-have compilation of unreleased songs and other forgotten recordings.

A story by Vincent Vanoli

drake

1948 – 1974

IT WAS DURING A NIGHT OF SOLITUDE THAT SHE CAME.

FROM A LOST OR MYTHICAL TIME, LIKE AN EGYPTIAN PRINCESS IN HER FINERY.

WHO ARE YOU? WHERE ARE YOU FROM? I DON'T KNOW YOU.

LET'S GO...

EVEN THOUGH I COME FROM FAR AWAY AND EVEN THOUGH I LIVED A LONG TIME AGO, YOU KNOW ME.

WHERE ARE THE MYTHS, WHAT BECAME OF THOSE PRECIOUS TRADITIONS, ONCE TINGED WITH GOLD AND MELANCHOLY?

GIVE ME SOMETHING THAT MAKES THIS MODERN WORLD WORTH THE TROUBLE.

I HAVE FIVE LEAVES LEFT.

"Summer was gone and the heat died down And Autumn reached for her golden crown

I looked behind as I heard a sigh But this was the time of no reply

The sun went down and the crowd went home

I was left by the roadside all alone.

I turned to speak as they went by

But this was the time of no reply.

The time of no reply is calling me to stay

There is no hello and no goodbye

To leave there is no way.

The trees on the hill
had nothing to say
They would keep their
dreams till another
day

So they stood and
thought and wondered
why For this was
the time of no
reply.

Time goes by
from year to
year And no
one asks why
I am standing
here.

But I have my
answer as I
look at the
sky

This is
the time
of no
reply."

Vanoli.

A gladiator in the arena before his audience: for Iggy Pop, concerts were theatrical performances without a safety net. At once an acrobat and a clown, a kamikaze pilot and mime, he brought danger and the strange to the stage, rolling in broken glass until he bled or covering himself with peanut butter. While others acted out horror, he was the real thing, offering his body as a sacrifice. But he needed a stage for his trances, and a soundtrack to match his furious actions. The other members of the Stooges provided the electrical spark, the special elixir of madness.

Before Ron and Scott, the Asheton brothers, turned to their instruments (the guitar and drums, respectively), a life on the fringe called to them. Until that point, these juvenile delinquents, drawn to Nazi imagery, didn't fit into any category—especially in Ann Arbor, Michigan. Thanks to The Who and the Stones, the two brothers saw that they could transcend lives destined for mediocrity by making the most intense noise possible. When they met James Osterberg, who would become Iggy Pop, their explosive, wild ways took shape. Now they had an envoy, a crazy and charismatic leader.

IGGY POP

BORN IN 1947

SELECTED DISCOGRAPHY

The Stooges (1969)
The first explosion, detonated with John Cale, formerly of the Velvet Underground.

Fun House (1970)
The Stooges in a free rock trance.

Raw Power (1973)
The last album of an incomparable trilogy that lays down the laws of punk.

The Idiot (1977)
Mutant and semi–New Wave metamorphosis in Berlin.

From 1969 to 1970 : The Stooges
From 1973 to 1977 : Iggy & The Stooges
After 1977 : Iggy Pop

A story by
Tanquerelle

And so, as it had for the more political MC5, Detroit became home to another apostle of heavy, powerful rock.

Osterberg, a blues fan, grew up in a trailer in Ann Arbor. In the mid-1960s, this drummer came back from a trip to Chicago convinced that it was pointless for a little white guy like himself to meticulously imitate his black mentors. A Doors

never gave a concert in anything other than an altered state. Carried away by the chaotic lifestyle that ruled over their den, the Fun House, the Stooges were saved by a good Samaritan named David Bowie (during the same period, he got Lou Reed back into the saddle with the album *Transformer*). Introducing himself to the wild and uncontrollable rocker that Iggy Pop embodied in the raw, the blond singer with the mismatched eyes took these nomads under his

A GLADIATOR IN THE ARENA BEFORE HIS AUDIENCE: FOR IGGY POP, CONCERTS WERE THEATRICAL PERFORMANCES WITHOUT A SAFETY NET

concert, with Jim Morrison striking an I-don't-give-a-damn attitude, was the trigger. Drawing on his frustrations, Iggy Pop strove to create his own direct and primitive language. Behind him were the Asheton brothers and the bassist Dave Alexander, who worked metal like blacksmiths. The day the Stooges signed with their label, they only had three real songs. The rest of what they played onstage was improvised. When they returned to their hotel, Ron Asheton spent an hour finding the screaming chords for several of their metallic classics, including "No Fun," which the Sex Pistols took on in 1977. Although their technique was pretty crude, the Stooges had big ambitions. Staggered by the free music of John Coltrane and Miles Davis, they introduced a saxophonist, Steve MacKay, in an attempt to embrace jazz without losing their fury.

Drugs caught up with the group, while Ron stayed clean, the others plummeted. Irresistible (the singer Nico was charmed) and ready for anything, Iggy popped acid daily, and had a hard time finding veins for shooting up. He

wing. At first, the combination failed: Bowie and his management ended up cutting them off, and Iggy asked to be admitted to a psychiatric hospital. But in the meantime, the Stooges, with new guitarist James Williamson, recorded the earth-shattering *Raw Power*, one of the favorite albums of the rock critic Lester Bangs. Its aftershock can still be felt decades later. In 1977, Iggy left for decadent Berlin to find Bowie; their intense friendship led to a fruitful comeback for the Stooges' ex-lead singer. Since then, Iggy has become clean and leads a healthy life. Singers that came after him (from Kurt Cobain of Nirvana to the White Stripes and Peaches) have looked to him as a guru, an incredible survivor. He still has inexhaustible energy on stage, especially since he reunited with the Asheton brothers to bring back the Stooges, playing together until Ron's death in January 2009. Hervé Tanquerelle tells us their wonderful story through an impressive array of alter egos.

PLAYLIST

1 1969 (1969)
2 I Wanna Be Your Dog (1969)
3 No Fun (1969)
4 Real Cool Time (1969)
5 Down on the Street (1970)
6 T.V. Eye (1970)
7 Dirt (1970)
8 I Got a Right (1973)
9 Search and Destroy (1973)
10 Gimme Danger (1973)
11 Raw Power (1973)
12 Nightclubbing (1977)
13 China Girl (1977)
14 Lust for Life (1977)
15 The Passenger (1977)
16 Some Weird Sin (1979)
17 Real Wild Child (Wild One) (1986)
18 Wild America (1993)
19 In the Deathcar (1993)
20 Corruption (1999)

ANN in the FUN HOUSE

1969... all across the USA. The young Ann began to feel very bored...

She was wondering if, in spite of the overwhelming heat, she should phone her mom, when all of a sudden...

In the early 1970s, when a group of American troublemakers decided to put on makeup, dress as women, wear high heels, and name themselves after a doll shop, you couldn't say they were like everyone else. The New York Dolls almost never wanted to fit the mold. Their spectacular career was marked by extreme extravagance, which attracted fans of decadence and theatricality, earned them a place in the spotlight—unsigned and without an album, they opened for Rod Stewart. And furthermore, by keeping their sexuality undefined, these complete heteros had more groupies than anyone else. Would David Bowie have played the bisexuality card with Ziggy Stardust and his other character without having seen them live first?

PLAYLIST

1 Personality Crisis (1973)
2 Looking for a Kiss (1973)
3 Frankenstein (1973)
4 Trash (1973)
5 Jet Boy (1973)
6 Endless Party (1973)
7 Babylon (1974)
8 Who Are the Mystery Girls? (1974)
9 Puss'n'Boots (1974)
10 Chatterbox (1974)
11 Born to Lose (1977)
12 Chinese Rocks (1977)
13 Pirate Love (1977)
14 You Can't Put Your Arms Round a Memory (1978)
15 London Boys (1978)
16 (She's so) Untouchable (1978)
17 Hurt Me (1983)
18 M.I.A. (1985)
19 Little Bit of Whore (1985)
20 Society Makes Me Sad (1991)

UNTIL HIS MYSTERIOUS DEATH, HE WAS A CHARISMATIC FIGURE, AN INIMITABLE SINGER-GUITARIST AND A WONDERFUL LOSER

While the group, in maintaining their image—glittery and outrageous—enormously influenced rock star fashion, the thundering rock that the New York Dolls played also made an impression. While nodding to their roots—the concise energy of rock pioneers, like Chuck Berry and Bo Diddley, the sensuality of Otis Redding's rhythm and blues—they paved the way of the future of punk and metal kitsch, like Kiss. These dolls were the most dominant gang of good-for-nothings around. David Johansen, their lead singer, was a younger and more provocative Jagger, and Johnny Thunders was a glam Keith Richards; then there was Sylvain Sylvain, the other flamboyant guitarist, Arthur "Killer" Kane on bass, and Jerry Nolan, the veteran, on drums. They weren't all hedonism and bawdiness, however. Early on, one of their members fell to drugs: Billy Murcia, Nolan's predecessor, lapsed into unconsciousness

during a party, having overdosed on alcohol and sedatives. He drowned in the bathtub that someone pushed him into. In 1975, Thunders and Nolan's addiction to heroin, in addition to the difficulties they had achieving recognition, were the main issues that tore the group apart. We should add that the last attempts of their English manager—the late Malcolm McLaren—to popularize them were also unfruitful. Oddly enough, he was nevertheless able to reform their nefarious sexual image with a radically different Communist Party theme (red with a hammer and sickle). In the United States, this wasn't going to work. Paradox: like other bands (Lou Reed's Velvet Underground, Iggy Pop's Stooges), the New York Dolls would crumble and fall once the shock of their appearance had faded, only to become legends later.

As the group gradually deteriorated, Johnny Thunders and Jerry Nolan abandoned the

SELECTED DISCOGRAPHY

New York Dolls (1973)
First thundering album, wild and sexy, instant classics.

Too Much Too Soon (1974)
Poppier (thanks to the producer of the girl band The Shangri-Las) but just as thrilling.

L.A.M.F. (1977)
A troublemaking punk album recorded with the Heartbreakers and good English spunk.

So Alone (1978)
More personal and introspective, ballads that will make you cry.

A story by Stéphane Oiry

From 1973 to 1974 : New York Dolls
1977 : Johnny Thunders and the Heartbreakers
After 1977 : Johnny Thunders

JOHNNY THUNDERS

1952 – 1991

other dolls to form the Heartbreakers, which for a while included Richard Hell—another American punk pioneer, and the creator of the flagrant *Blank Generation*. As fate would have it, the Heartbreakers went on tour with a few bands from the English punk scene that the New York Dolls had directly influenced. Among them were the notorious Sex Pistols, whose crazy career was managed by Malcolm McLaren, who was better able to control them. Up until his mysterious death in 1991 in New Orleans, where he hoped to record an acoustic album, Johnny Thunders was a charismatic figure, an inimitable singer-guitarist, and a wonderful loser. Sometimes sublime, often erratic, the concerts he gave toward the end of his life—like the one described by Stéphane Oiry—depended on his state at that moment. Despite his attempts to stay clean, Thunders lost his battle with dope, his most loyal companion that kept him hooked for fifteen years. Like Chet Baker in jazz, an accomplice in addiction, he rode a rollercoaster in his last years, plunging down into rocker junkydom and occasionally coming up for air. That said, when three original band members got the New York Dolls back together in 2004 (releasing an album two years later), it added nothing to the legend.

BORN TO LOSE

BY STÉPHANE OIRY

MY NAME IS MANU. FOR ALMOST TWO MONTHS NOW, I'VE BEEN SQUATTING AT ALAIN'S, WHO'S A REAL FAG. ALAIN IS A BIT OLDER THAN ME. I MET HIM IN A BAR, I DIDN'T HAVE A PLACE TO STAY. HE SAID TO ME, "MY PLACE IS SMALL, BUT I'M HARDLY EVER THERE. YOU'LL BE COMFORTABLE."

IT'S TRUE THE BASTARD IS NEVER THERE. HE SPENDS HIS DAYS AT THE MOVIES WRITING ARTICLES, "REVIEWS" HE CALLS THEM, FOR A RAG.

HIS PLACE IS GRIMY, BUT IT'S OK: THERE ARE BOOKS TO READ, PILES OF VIDEOS TO WATCH, SOME TUNES.

ALAIN IS ALWAYS BROKE. SOMETIMES HIS MOTHER COMES BY TO FILL THE FRIDGE. SHE GETS ME DOWN, THAT WOMAN. ESPECIALLY SINCE I'M THE ONE THAT HAS TO MAKE CONVERSATION WITH HER. IT'S BAD. I REALLY DON'T KNOW WHAT TO SAY!

DAMN! IT'S COLD! I ONLY HAVE A T-SHIRT ON UNDER THIS.

HE'S OFTEN LIKE THAT, MEAN, ARROGANT. HE WANTS MY ASS. HE WOULD LIKE TO FUCK ME. I DON'T WANT TO. THAT'S NOT MY THING. REALLY, I DON'T WANT TO!

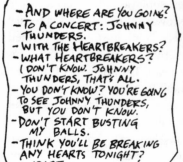

- AND WHERE ARE YOU GOING?
- TO A CONCERT: JOHNNY THUNDERS.
- WITH THE HEARTBREAKERS?
- WHAT HEARTBREAKERS? I DON'T KNOW. JOHNNY THUNDERS, THAT'S ALL.
- YOU DON'T KNOW? YOU'RE GOING TO SEE JOHNNY THUNDERS, BUT YOU DON'T KNOW.
- DON'T START BUSTING MY BALLS.
- THINK YOU'LL BE BREAKING ANY HEARTS TONIGHT? IDIOT.

WE'RE HERE TO SEE JOHNNY, NOT SOME BLONDE CHICK SINGING INSTEAD.

NORMAL PEOPLE, I MEAN WITH A HEALTHY LIBIDO, MIGHT NOT NEED MORE THAN THIS PAIR OF TITS. NOT ME.

IT'S THE BIG WHATEVER. ALAIN WOULD KNOW HOW TO DESCRIBE IT. WORDS ARE HIS JOB. BLA, BLA, BLAH...

SHE'S DRIVING US CRAZY.

HER SHRILL, ROTTEN VOICE IS DRIVING US CRAZY. AND THAT SMELL OF VOMIT, BEER, AND SHIT COMBINED.

NEXT TO ME A SCARY DUDE IS YELLING, "GO TO HELL, JOHNNY, GO TO HELL!" THERE'S SOMETHING WRONG WITH THAT IDIOT.

I'M IN THE FRONT ROW.

JOHNNY LOOKS HORRIBLE. HIS CHEEKS ARE HOLLOW AND HE'S GOT ALL KINDS OF YELLOW SPOTS ON HIS SKIN.

LOOKS LIKE PISS, LIKE SOME- ONE PISSED ON HIS FACE AND THE URINE ATE INTO HIS SKIN. SHIT, WHAT A DUMB IDEA. HOW DID I COME UP WITH THAT?

IF I'M NOT CAREFUL, I'M GONNA GET KICKED IN THE FACE. PLUS THE BASTARD IS SPITTING ON US.

YUCK.

I NEVER SAW SUCH A CRAZY CONCERT.

THAT'S FOR SURE!

THERE SHE IS, THAT GIRL, A CHICK I SOMETIMES SEE AT CONCERTS. SHE HANGS WITH WEIRD GUYS.

HE DOESN'T SOUND SO HOT, OLD MAN JOHNNY!

YOU LIKED IT. I SAW YOU!

I SAW HER ONE DAY WITH THOSE GUYS BY THE CANAL. I THINK THEY'RE SQUATTING AROUND THERE.

HIS VOICE IS UNRECOGNIZABLE, HE SOUNDS LIKE A LITTLE BOY WHOSE VOICE HASN'T BROKEN YET.

AND YOU LIKE IT, DON'T YOU!

– DID HE PLAY "CHINESE ROCKS"?
– UM... I DON'T THINK SO, NO.
– YEAH, YEAH, BUT IT WAS A WASH-OUT, WEAK, SUNG LIKE A SOW.
– WOW, SO YOUR EAR IS GOOD ENOUGH TO MAKE OUT THE NOTES COMING OUT OF HIS SNOUT, OINK OINK!
– ANYWAY, "CHINESE ROCKS" ISN'T ONE OF HIS SONGS.
– WHAT DO YOU MEAN "CHINESE ROCKS" ISN'T HIS! IT'S ON "L.A.M.F."!
– MAYBE, BUT IT WAS ORIGINALLY WRITTEN BY DEE DEE RAMONE FOR RICHARD HELL.

SHE HAS A TATTOO AT THE NAPE OF HER NECK, IT SAYS SOMETHING BUT I CAN'T MAKE IT OUT.

HOW DO YOU KNOW THAT?

I JUST DO. DEE DEE TOLD ME.

IT ALWAYS DOES SOMETHING TO ME, SEEING THAT GIRL! SHE'S SO FRAGILE, I FEEL BAD.

DEE DEE TOLD YOU, HA HA!

YOU'RE AN IDIOT.

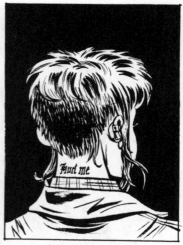

SHIT, IS THAT BEER COMING, OR WHAT?

SHE STEPS AWAY FROM THE BAR AND HER FRIENDS. I FOLLOW HER, FIRST WITH MY EYES. SHE MOVES HER HEAD IN A WAY I TAKE TO BE AN INVITATION, OR MAYBE I'M IMAGINING IT...
I WALK BEHIND HER FOR A LONG TIME. WE'RE IN THE COURTYARD NOW, IT'S DARK. SHE SEEMS NOT TO CARE THAT I'M EVEN THERE. THE WALLS ARE COVERED WITH OBSCENITIES AND THE NAMES OF GROUPS THAT HAVE PLAYED THERE.

"HURT ME."

THANKS TO APPOLLO FOR HIS INVOLUNTARY HELP.

A perky blonde, Blondie was the creation of Chic Young, the American cartoonist who made a name for himself with a comic strip about a family. His characters, Blondie Boopadoop and her husband, Dagwood Bumstead, were the model couple that never aged. The heroine symbolized the ideal average American household: simple but stylish, always elegant and cared for. Debbie Harry, who alone represents the group Blondie, is an equivalent symbol—but steamier: She is America's sweetheart. Embodying the average American girl (she worked as a secretary and a waitress at Max's Kansas City, the legendary New York nightclub and restaurant), Debbie has been the fantasy of countless virgin teenagers who played with her in Barbie form—they tacked her up on their bedroom walls, forever hoping to run into this (fake) blonde on the street. The focus on Debbie isn't meant to insult Chris Stein, the band's guitarist and, truth be told, the beauty's boyfriend; or Clem Burke (drums) and Jimmy Destri (keyboard), not to mention the string of bassists (Gary Valentine, Frank Infante, Nigel Harrison). But, no matter your sex, she's the one you end up devouring with your eyes; she's a poster girl with a charming voice, the perfect pop icon. While they posed as a group for their album covers—Stanislas Gros tells a story about their third album cover, *Parallel Lines*—the singles only displayed her beauty: Debbie, a vamp in a black dress, defying the buyer; Debbie in a leopard outfit (the cover for "Denis"), etc. She first played in a typical three-person girl group, but ended up creating a girl band full of boys.

From the start, in the mid-1970s, despite her sweet, polite looks, Blondie was part of the tumultuous New York scene that wanted to break free from the past and subvert rock to give it new life. Rock and its elder members had become lazy in the comforts of success. Debbie's band shared the stage with the Ramones, who shaped American punk, playing at underground clubs like CBGB's, which has since become a myth and a brand. More experimental bands—like Television, Talking

PLAYLIST

1 X Offender (1976)
2 In the Flesh (1976)
3 Rip Her to Shreds (1976)
4 Denis (1977)
5 (I'm Always Touched by Your) Presence Dear (1977)
6 Hanging on the Telephone (1978)
7 One Way or Another (1978)
8 Picture This (1978)
9 Fade Away and Radiate (1978)
10 I Know But I Don't Know (1978)
11 Sunday Girl (1978)
12 Heart of Glass (1978)
13 Dreaming (1979)
14 Union City Blue (1979)
15 Die Young Stay Pretty (1979)
16 Atomic (1979)
17 Rapture (1980)
18 The Tide Is High (1980)
19 Island of Lost Souls (1982)
20 Maria (1999)

Heads, and Johnny Thunders' Heartbreakers— were also part of the shake-up. An integral member of this incestuous movement, in which groups hooked up and broke up like friends and lovers, Blondie, an apostle to a lesser degree, represented the poppier and more playful side. Their songs tamed electricity; Debbie's voice carries the melody, and the arrangements wink a barely ironic eye to the carefree bubblegum pop of the sixties (Phil Spector's productions and his famous Wall of Sound, the Shangri-Las, etc.). "Denis," for example, one of the group's biggest hits, categorized by default as New Wave, is a masculine cover of "Denise," a hit by the obscure rhythm and blues band Randy & the Rainbows. One of Blondie's strengths is their ability to effortlessly embrace every style of popular music, the kind that plays on the radio. After looking back to naïve 1960s rock, the group quickly took on

> **ONE OF BLONDIE'S STRENGTHS IS THEIR ABILITY TO EFFORTLESSLY EMBRACE EVERY STYLE OF POPULAR MUSIC**

the rhythms of disco ("Heart of Glass" and "Call Me," composed by one of the masters of the genre, the Italian Giorgio Moroder, who wrote the torrid "Love to Love You Baby" and "I Feel Love" for Donna Summer) and also reggae ("The Tide Is High," a cover). They were the first American pop band to borrow the trendiest genre of 1980, hip hop, for "Rapture," a clever stylistic appropriation that is half pastiche. This frenzy of new sensations coincided with a growing lack of conviction and cohesion, though. After the catastrophic *The Hunter* (1982), Debbie disbanded the group and launched her solo career . . . but was never as charismatic as she was when she played with Chris Stein and his cohorts. Hence their reunion in the late 1980s, which was neither glorious nor completely shameful. Blondie's own influence has not waned, and, from Courtney Love to Madonna—not forgetting Garbage—countless musicians have turned to her.

Blondie

FORMED IN 1975

A story by Stanislas Gros

SELECTED DISCOGRAPHY

Blondie (1976)
A testament to the group's early period, borne out of the upheaval of punk and New Wave.

Plastic Letters (1977)
The New Yorkers posed on a borrowed police car for the cover. This fueled-up album contains their first hit ("Denis").

Parallel Lines (1978)
The perfect blend of sophisticated pop with a carefree spirit, bordering on disco.

Blondie

IN 1978, PARALLEL LINES WAS RELEASED. IT WAS BLONDIE'S THIRD ALBUM, AND THE FIRST OF THEIR THREE BIG SUCCESSES, ALONG WITH EAT TO THE BEAT AND AUTOAMERICAN.

ITS VERY FAMOUS COVER PRESENTS THE SINGER, DEBBIE HARRY, STANDING WITH HER GROUP IN FRONT OF A BACKGROUND OF BLACK VERTICAL STRIPES.

YES DEBBIE, WHAT IS IT?

OH, CHRIS...

WELL NOTHING... AM I ON MY OWN? WHERE'S THE REST OF THE GROUP?

THE REST OF THE GROUP? WHY?

I DON'T KNOW... TO PLAY MUSIC MAYBE...

OH, OH, MUSIC... WELL, THEY SHOULD BE AROUND HERE SOMEWHERE...

129

IN 1981, DEBBIE HARRY'S FIRST SOLO ALBUM WAS RELEASED Koo Koo

THE ALBUM'S ARTWORK WAS CREATED BY GIGER, WHO HAD JUST DESIGNED THE MONSTERS FOR THE MOVIE ALIEN.

THE ALBUM COVER SHOWED DEBBIE'S FACE PIERCED BY METAL SPEARS, AND WAS SO SHOCKING THAT THE NEW YORK CITY SUBWAY REFUSED TO ADVERTISE IT.

ON THE NET, IT'S PRETTY EASY TO FIND THE AMAZING VIDEOS "BACKFIRED" AND "NOW I KNOW YOU KNOW."

THIS ODD ALBUM COMBINES FUNK, ROCK, REGGAE, AND EVEN RAP, AND HAS AGED VERY WELL, I THINK. AT THE TIME, HOWEVER, THE PUBLIC AND CRITICS PANNED IT. BLONDIE'S AND DEBBIE'S CAREERS NEVER FULLY RECOVERED.

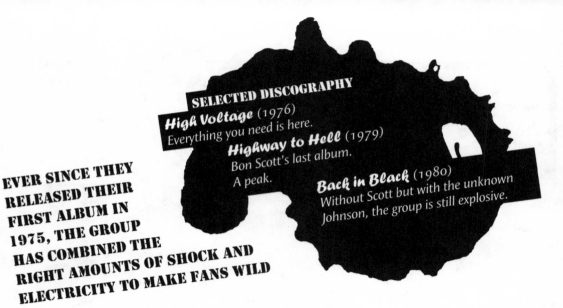

EVER SINCE THEY RELEASED THEIR FIRST ALBUM IN 1975, THE GROUP HAS COMBINED THE RIGHT AMOUNTS OF SHOCK AND ELECTRICITY TO MAKE FANS WILD

If dinosaurs had heard AC/DC, maybe they would have survived the shocks of climate change and evolution. Seemingly unaffected by the erosion of time, this Australian group, Stephen King's baby, has withstood the shifting tides of fashion and the passing of decades. In sports it would be foolish to change a winning team, an adage that AC/DC has made its own. Ever since they released their first album in 1975, the group has combined the right amount of shock and electricity to make fans wild, mixing together huge guitar riffs and loud energy with a love for the crude and lewd. They've never strayed from this first explosive recipe. They would certainly have set a record in longevity had there charismatic singer, Bon Scott, not died an untimely death. But his passing in February 1980 did not undermine the determination of the surviving band members. How could they lose momentum after finding the magic, untouchable formula for a kind of hard rock that was singed with blues, and as juicy as forbidden fruit? The show must go on. So the Young brothers, Angus and Malcolm, the two guitarists, found a replacement and kept the machine running. Brian Johnson, the cap-wearing car lover, has played the part since *Back in Black* (1980), an homage without tears. AC/DC is the last bastion of bawdy rock, catering to hormones while remaining loyal to the ways of the past (attached to the notion

of albums, the group refuses to sell its songs individually in the digital world).

At first, it was a family matter. The Young kids, born in Scotland, moved to Australia in the early 1960s. When he invited his younger brothers, Malcolm and Andy, to help in the studio during recording sessions, the older brother, George, a guitarist for the Easybeats (a successful pop band), passed on the fever. Later, he became coproducer and helped the budding group create rock-solid first albums. And Margaret, the older sister, was the one who spotted the initials AC/DC on a household appliance (meaning alternating current/direct current) and suggested that her brothers adopt this ambiguous abbreviation. She also advised Angus to wear his schoolboy uniform, a costume that, although now a gimmick, did a lot for the group's image—as did Bon Scott's clown garb. Scott was full of charm and had devastating sex appeal. As Appollo and Brüno show in the pages that follow—hardly romanticizing the matter—Scott was the leader of the pack when he was in the group. And yet he wasn't the Young brothers' first choice. He was a quick replacement for their first singer, who had been thrown out. Before he joined the band, Scott had already had quite a life. A member of a few obscure Australian groups, he always lived his life to the fullest. Deemed "socially maladjusted" by the army, his rap

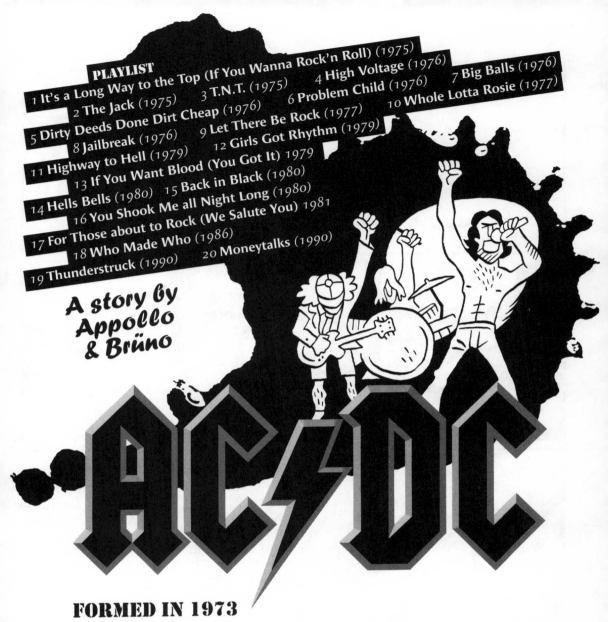

A story by Appollo & Brüno

FORMED IN 1973

sheet was far from clean. To earn a living, he even worked as a diver and a fisherman. The Young brothers spotted him when he was their chauffeur. In a voice warmed by alcohol, this hedonist and jester lent a heavy sexual tone to AC/DC's songs, often with bawdy double entendres. For example, "The Jack," which describes a poker game, also describes how the narrator caught a venereal disease; "Whole Lotta Rosie" tells of a girl without inhibitions—Scott is said to have been inspired by one of his girlfriends who, in a single month, is said to have slept with more than thirty guys. In the key

song, "Highway to Hell," the singer goes so far as to establish a parallel between hedonism and damnation. And he does so without knowing that several months later he would choke on his own vomit and be found lifeless in a car, a victim of his unhinged ways. After a warning in 1979 and after having his stomach pumped before a concert, Scott knew his life was on its last legs. But he made light of it, and was driven by the raw energy of AC/DC's music, which, despite all its imitators (Guns N' Roses, for example) still strikes a chord. It makes the teenager in every rock fan vibrate, even if only for a moment.

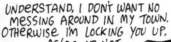

SHIT, BROTHER, HER SKIN IS LIKE SATIN, HER LIPS TASTE LIKE STRAWBERRIES...

AND HER TITS, JESUS, HER TITS!

SHIT, WHAT'S THIS?

HUH?

IT'S THE SHERIFF, HE'S TELLING ME TO PULL OVER.

SHIT, THAT'S MY FATHER!

YOUR FATHER? THE SHERIFF IS YOUR FATHER???

YUP, DUDE.

I'M ARRESTING YOU FOR OBSCENE BEHAVIOR IN PUBLIC.

JUDY, GO HOME RIGHT AWAY!

I HAVEN'T DONE ANYTHING! GET ME OUT OF HERE!

I HAVE THE RIGHT TO DETAIN YOU FOR 24 HOURS, AND I INTEND TO DO SO. I'M NOT BUDGING FROM HERE, AND YOU WON'T EITHER, BELIEVE ME.

OH BONNY, I'M SO HAPPY WE HAVE SOME TIME TOGETHER.

WE HAVE 24 HOURS, HONEY.

YES...

APPOLLO-BRÜNO

FIN

How were four scary-looking guys in leather jackets able to change the history of rock with such limited technique and with songs all cast from the same basic mold? Despite having artistic ambitions that bordered on nothingness, the Ramones revolutionized rock and roll by democratizing it. Their emergence in New York in the mid-1970s proved that anyone could get up onstage and show rage. No need to know music theory or the classics: you just had to have enough frustration to keep you going, an energy that transcended anonymity and gave it a voice. Joey (vocals), Johnny (guitar), Dee Dee (bass), and Tommy (drums)—who, after a few years, was replaced by Marky—were certainly frustrated. Psychiatric hospitals, heroin, and addiction ever since adolescence, the absence of family support, the hustling . . . This group of would-be brothers, pure products of the middle class,

bonded over a common feeling of rejection. Hence the negativity and aggression of their songs—like bricks through windows.

The first album by the Ramones is a real, brutal, and direct statement about their dirty and entirely unglamorous aesthetic. Posing in front of a gray wall for the cover, they come clean about their modest intentions. For two minutes at most, their songs, like riots, combine basic, unstoppable, superfast guitar chords with nihilistic slogan lyrics. Heirs of the New York Dolls and Iggy Pop's Stooges, they are extremists of the short and abrupt. Their mini-hymns, systematically introduced by Dee Dee counting off "One, two, three, four," are slices of raw life: kids overcome boredom by sniffing glue; a former green beret turned prostitute kills his client; a mother chases her child with a bat.

Intentionally improper, interjecting a Nazi verse for shock value,

A story by Sébastien Lumineau

RAMONES

1974 – 1996

the brotherhood that was the Ramones fit in perfectly with the New York rock family. At CBGB's they played alongside Blondie, Television, and others. And because these Beagle Boys (almost) never strayed from their formula, which was as sharp as

THE RAMONES WERE, IN FACT, THE PUNK OFFSPRING OF THE BEATLES OR THE BEACH BOYS

the Flintstones, there was time enough to get past their looks and dirty ways (like when they would piss in their guests' glasses backstage) and realize that the Ramones were, in fact, the punk offspring of the Beatles or the Beach Boys. Even covered with guitar spikes, they favored melody and pop immediacy, just as their elders had. Phil Spector, the legendary producer and capricious hit-maker, played it right: in 1979, at a time when the Ramones were guest stars in the movie *Rock n' Roll High School*, he took them under his wing to record the very 1960's *End of Century*. Surreal scenes followed, like when Spector held the group at gunpoint for a whole day!

Over the next two decades, the group staved off fatigue; but at the beginning of the millennium, the men were reminded that they weren't indestructible. In just a few years Joey, Dee Dee (he had left the band long before), and Johnny died. Their influence is nevertheless strong, and they are responsible for countless other bands; English punks that started in 1976, like the Clash, for one. But they've also inspired bands like Metallica, neo-punks like Green Day, and brainier rockers like Sonic Youth. The Ramones were as triumphant as a virus: the same band that started out on the fringe came to infect popular culture. "Hey, ho, let's go," the refrain from "Blitzkrieg Bop," was adopted as a stadium chant, and their logo (an American eagle with a bat) appears on every kind of clothing . . . even for children. Not only does Sébastien Lumineau revive Joey, Johnny, and Dee Dee for us, but he immerses us into their lives on tour—so fast, you couldn't even count to four.

SELECTED DISCOGRAPHY

Ramones (1976)
The essence of the group.
Their first album is a punch.

Rocket to Russia (1977)
For their third album in less than two years, the Ramones didn't change their formula. The classics are here.

It's Alive (1979)
Recorded on New Year's Eve 1977, with the would-be brothers on stage singing more than thirty songs in a row within an hour.

End of a Century (1980)
What happens when the Ramones meet Phil Spector.

PLAYLIST

1 **Blitzkrieg Bop** (1976)
2 **Beat on the Brat** (1976)
3 **Judy Is a Punk** (1976)
4 **Now I Wanna Sniff some Glue** (1976)
5 **53rd and 3rd** (1976)
6 **Gimme Gimme Shock Treatment** (1977)
7 **Sheena Is a Punk Rocker** (1977)
8 **Suzy Is a Headbanger** (1977)
9 **Pinhead** (1977)   10 **Cretin Hop** (1977)
11 **Rockaway Beach** (1977)
12 **We're a Happy Family** (1977)
13 **Teenage Lobotomy** (1977)
14 **I Wanna Be Sedated** (1978)
15 **Do You Remember Rock'n Roll Radio?** (1980)
16 **Chinese Rock** (1980)
17 **Rock'n Roll High School** (1980)
18 **The KKK Took My Baby Away** (1981)
19 **Too Tough to Die** (1985)
20 **What a Wonderful World** (2002) Joey Ramone

AND NOW, THE RAMONES!

SÉBASTIEN LUMINEAU

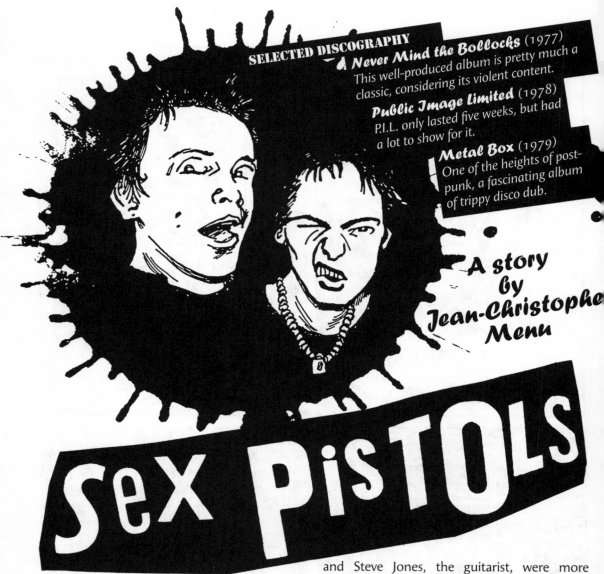

A story by Jean-Christophe Menu

SeX PiSTOLs

FORMED IN 1975

It took a few insults hurled at the presenter Bill Grundy during a television program on December 1, 1976, for the Sex Pistols to come to embody evil in the eyes of conservative England. Until then, the group was only gently provocative and clearly lucrative for the band's manager, Malcolm McLaren. Coming back from New York, he had decided to import the rebellious spirit and look of the first American punk bands (the Ramones, Richard Hell). The bassist, Glen Matlock actually preferred the Beatles to chaos; and Paul Cook, the drummer,

and Steve Jones, the guitarist, were more interested in getting laid than in overturning the system. In fact, only John Lydon had what it took to worry the leaders of a country in turmoil, upended by unemployment and racism. Having auditioned in the S&M clothing boutique run by McLaren and Vivienne Westwood, Lydon gave the group its real subversive flavor. The others had the equipment—some of it stolen by Jones during a Bowie concert—but not much more than a will to play basic rock and roll. Because he didn't give a damn about fame and the system, because he found his clothes in the trash, Lydon—renamed Rotten because of his teeth—had the right attitude. Above all, he wrote incendiary and sarcastic lyrics that

1977 : The Sex Pistols
Starting in 1978 : P.I.L.,
except "My Way" : Sid Vicious

ONLY JOHN LYDON HAD WHAT IT TOOK TO WORRY THE LEADERS OF A COUNTRY IN TURMOIL, UPENDED BY UNEMPLOYMENT AND RACISM

violent behavior. The Pistols signed with three labels, one after the other, and McLaren secured an incredible advance each time. In June 1977, with the Queen's jubilee in full swing, the group boarded a barge to celebrate the release of the disrespectful "God Save the Queen," but were quickly arrested. It became absurd: the single, banned from the airwaves, was number one on the charts but didn't appear there because of censorship. The Pistols' status as public enemy clashed with reality: at Christmas, the group played at a gala for the children of firemen (then on strike). Vicious became involved in a toxic relationship with American Nancy Sprungen, who introduced him to drugs and addiction.

"Ever get the feeling you've been cheated?" With this question, uttered on January 14, 1978, in San Francisco, a disgusted John Lydon ended the last concert of a disastrous American tour that lay bare the discord between the destitute Pistols and their clever manager. It wasn't long before the singer showed another face. Far from wanting to start a new chapter (as McLaren, a master of media manipulation, had suggested), Lydon was, in fact, cultivated, a fan of Oscar Wilde and interested in deviant music (Captain Beefheart, Can). Once at the center of English punk, he quickly launched into post-punk with Public Image Limited (P.I.L.), founded with Keith Levene, the talented guitarist who had left the Clash, and John Wardle, the bassist now named Jah Wobble. A shared fascination with reggae, dub, and experimental sound bonded the trio together. In 1979, a few months after Sid Vicious had died of an overdose (he was suspected in the murder of Sprungen at the end of 1978), P.I.L. even took disco in a conceptual direction. The original trio later disbanded, and Lydon stood alone. But the Sex Pistols, who proclaimed "No Future," reunited as early as 1996. Jean-Christophe Menu takes a look at when he discovered the group, in a special issue of his *Lockgroove Comix*.

scandalized the prudish majority—taking abortion or the Queen as subjects, as he did for 'God Save the Queen,' a genuine crime of lèse-majesté. His contemptuous and sneering voice transformed near rhymes ("antichrist" and "anarchist" in "Anarchy in the UK") into nihilist battle cries.

The day after the Grundy show, the tabloids went wild—one of the headlines "The Filth and the Fury" is now legendary. The group became the prey of an excessive witch hunt. Because he was too nice, Matlock was replaced by Sid Vicious; a buddy of Lydon, he was a big fan of the group and invented the pogo. His little talent as a bassist was overwhelmed by his

"...and Jesus Lizard?

OH NO

Laughing Hyenas? The Cows?

NO NO

OK, I'll go with the Sex Pistols

OK

OK, I've read VERMOREL's book three times (published in 1978 by Humanoïdes Associés as part of the collection SPEED 17), and I read through JON SAVAGE's entire tome ENGLAND'S DREAMING. Both are must-read books on the subject.

I must have a dozen live concerts, mostly pirated, including the last concert in SAN FRANCISCO on January 14, 1978

And even one from 2002 that's entirely respectable.

Which includes, I'll remind you, a cover of "SILVER MACHINE" by HAWKWIND, a song from 1972 sung by Lemmy...

But what's more important are these original 45s...

These original 45s were key to my discovery of the Pistols

Well, almost original

In 1977, I was 13, so no, I wasn't punk. I'm guessing that my first contact with punk was through the media, like it was for everyone...

bla bla punk bla bla England bla bla ha ha

Well aren't they handsome! Whatever will we see next!

I remember seeing a photo, something like this, in my parent's magazine. I was totally horrified!

PUNKS IN THE STREETS OF LONDON

②

The media scaring people any way they can isn't just a contemporary phenomenon.

PUNK = INSECURITY

So because I was living in the topographical bubble that is the suburbs of PARIS, punk was nothing but a distant threat.

Nevertheless, to everyone's surprise, there was soon a punk at my middle school. His name was Christophe L, and he was copying his big brother.

At the time, I was some kind of cheap hippie, and I considered myself to be a rebel. For me, dressing punk meant turning into a kind of clown.

Little by little, other students were contaminated by the phenomenon. Among them, Jean-Marc R., one of my oldest friends.

WHAT, YOU?! YOU'RE A P...PUNK?!

But all this didn't happen in '77. With the suburban lag, it must have been '79...

Hey look at R., He's "PUNK"!

HA! Idiot!

I knew him well, and one day at his house he wanted to introduce me to the SEX PISTOLS.

Listen to this!

MY WAY...

But that's horrible

Yeah, but wait, he's massacring the song on purpose!

Oh yeah?

I wasn't convinced, to say the least.

Rotten means "POURRI"! And Vicious is "vicieux"!!!

And the others?

No, Cook and Jones are their names.

Well that sucks!

GOD SAVE THE QUEEN! THE FASCIST REGIME!!

!?

Jean-Marc R. introduced punk and the SEX PISTOLS to me in a weird light.

Did you see Sid Vicious' T-shirt here?! HA HA!

Huh?

So Jean-Mark R. was one of those shady pseudo-punks who interpreted things in their own ways...

PUNK
US

It really reminded me of his infatuation when we were little. He was crazy about carpeting and soldiers, but especially from World War II.

TAKATAK!!
You don't want to play?

Nah

None of it gave me such a glowing picture of the SEX PISTOLS.

I preferred listening to real music!!

And the lamb... lies down... on Broadway!

GENESIS

But once I went with R. to "the" record store in town. He was waiting for something for weeks.

It arrived!

AAAAH!

This "collector's" item included six 45s in clear plastic cases.

The album information provided by John Savage tells me that the "SEX PACK" dates from December 1980. So it came out pretty late.

Which overlapped with the coming election in May 1981: some time in the months before, Jean-Mark R. became a member of the "Giscard d'Estaing youth"...

What the hell are you doing with that in your room?!

Well, we don't like Arabs, right mom?

GISCARD

That's for sure.

(a "black-foot" family, they were French colonists chased out of Algeria...)

In the meantime, R. had lent me some of his SEX PISTOLS 45s.

You sure?

Yeah, I don't listen to them so much anymore.

And that's when they started to become vaguely interesting to me.

?!!

SO PRETTY VACANT

So I think it was because R. was slowly becoming a fascist (and it must have only gotten worse) that I never returned his 45s to him...

Hey, you still have my SEX PISTOLS records?

Yeah, yeah, I'll get them back to you.

In short, R. became a fascist and I stopped hanging out with him. Thinking about him, I often remember the DEAD KENNEDYS' SONG "NAZI PUNKS FUCK OFF!"

But my real awakening about the SEX PISTOLS came later... when I bought a second-hand copy of NEVER MIND THE BOLLOCKS. Then I understood.

Oh, OK...

E.M.i.!

This was '82. Alice Cooper led me to the STRANGLERS and the CURE, and it was through New Wave that PUNK caught up with me. It had to.

So what?

When Jean-Marc R. made me listen to the PISTOLS 45s at his house, there was also this one from PUBLIC IMAGE LIMITED.

DEATH DISCO

I have it, but I don't know if it's the one that belonged to R. or if I bought it (must have, it's in great shape...)

What a record! And what a group!

PIL is a group that has had tremendous influence and is scandalously underrated. Maybe because it's hard to admit that the lead singer of a historically significant group could have done it again in another band that was just as important?

PiL

And then, in the category of records as objects, there's the METAL BOX (1978)!

And FLOWERS OF ROMANCE is one of my favorite albums of all time.

So, dear Readers, John LYDON is a very great man but not only because of the SEX PISTOLS.

Otherwise, I think that the best SEX PISTOLS concert was the one in DALLAS on JANUARY 10, 1978 (not only because Rotten called Texans cowboys and faggots)

I've got it on vinyl, you know! I guess you can find it on the internet, but I really don't care. ⑤

and to end: Jem's U.K. PUNK 77 FAVORITES

WIRE. Pink Flag, chairs missing, 154: the must-have trilogy. The barest means convey subtlety and subversion.

UNDERTONES. The first album, for example, or Hypnotised or the Peel Sessions. "Teenage Kicks," yes, but also "LISTENING IN".

ADVERTS: Crossing the red Sea with the Adverts. A few singles (GARY GILMORE'S EYES) and a perfect album, and it was over. Punk.

SWELL MAPS. A trip to Marineville or Jane From Occupied Europe. The most experimental and unique records. Still punk? I say yes.

999. The first album, melodic punk full of joyful hits. There wasn't anything afterward. Punk ?...

EATER. the youngest Punks in London in '77. A completely fresh take, brilliantly effective and then it was over. Punk!

THE FALL. The compilation of early singles, for example. But it's not over! A huge discography! Long live the Fall and MARK E. Smith!

REZILLOS. the Scottish answer to punk: festive, S.F., sixties, and pleasurable. The B52s stole everything from them. The SATELLITES owe something to them also!

BUZZCOCKS. Singles going steady. The best collection of punk-pop hits there is. What do I get? Everybody's happy nowadays.

All of this was made possible by:

N-ever mind the Bollocks

forever!

Although the Clash was part of punk in its early years, the group naturally strayed from the genre, not only to avoid the ritual of being spat at in the face, but also to advocate a musical shift that mocked the supposed values of the movement (being amateur, incompetent). The history of the group is nevertheless tied to the turbulence in London during the summer of 1976, at a time when the Sex Pistols were the leaders of nihilism. The son of a foreign-service diplomat, John Graham Mellor, aka Joe Strummer, had a real epiphany one night when he was part of a lineup that included the Pistols. The group, masterminded by Malcolm McLaren, was opening for the 101ers, the energetic but academic pub-rock band for which Strummer's voice was essential. That night, filled with fury and nerve, the Pistols struck the band that would soon be the Clash. Strummer immediately considered the 101ers as a thing of the past. When Mick Jones, already a good guitarist, and Paul Simonon, who became the bass guitarist, fell into his lap, the gang was born. Addressing unemployment and protest, the Clash's first songs rang in a return to the roots of rock and roll (simplicity, energy, a provocative spirit), a reaction to the direction in which the rock stars of the late 1970s had strayed. In terms of looks, they were adamant about their DIY stance, donning paint-splashed clothes that had less to do with Jackson Pollock than a need to repaint their digs. The Pistols' smack of heresy accounted for the rest: the Clash joined the Anarchy Tour, which ended after three concerts because it was too scandalous for Margaret Thatcher's uptight and racist England.

ADDRESSING UNEMPLOYMENT AND PROTEST, THE CLASH'S FIRST SONGS RANG IN A RETURN TO THE ROOTS OF ROCK AND ROLL

The English label CBS quickly signed the group (and thereby signaled the death of punk, according to one fanzine from the time). With their first album, recorded with the initial drummer Terry Chimes, the Clash established its ties to Jamaican reggae, covering the classic "Police and Thieves," which was a smash success at the last Notting Hill

THE
FUTURE
IS
UNWRITTEN

KNOW YOUR RIGHTS

A story by
Olivier
Josso

the CLASH

1976 – 1985

Carnival in 1976. A first for a white band.

Joined by the excellent Topper Headon at the barrels, the Londoners then discovered the United States, entering into an ambiguous relationship with the country. On one hand, they were inspired by its musical heritage, bringing the greats of rock and R&B on tour with them (Bo Diddley, Sam & Dave); on the other, they denounced American imperialism. After their masterpiece *London Calling* (featuring Simonon smashing his bass guitar, like an icon), they recorded a part of *Sandinista!* in the United States. Even more varied, and bordering on hip hop, which was echoing through the streets of New York, this triple album served as a gigantic laboratory. Although its miscellany was misunderstood, the intense crossbreeding of *Sandinista!* influenced upcoming generations of musicians and bands from Massive Attack to Manu Chao, not to mention Damon Albarn (Blur, Gorillaz). The Clash's relationship with America reached its public peak when the group, with two hits to their name ("Should I Stay or Should I Go" and "Rock the Casbah"),

opened for The Who at a stadium concert. This summit also signaled their downfall. Promiscuity and fatigue stirred tensions within the group: the guitarist Mick Jones was thrown out, just as Topper Headon had been, after he had become a junky. While Jones formed Big Audio Dynamite, a group falling between rock and dance, Joe Strummer and Paul Simonon recruited two guitarists to stand in for him before recording the aptly named *Cut the Crap*. The group's breakup was announced in early 1986: it would be an irrevocable decision. The group never got together again, respecting the code of honor they had established. Its members never sold out, and proved to be generous to their fans, providing rooms for a few of them and lowering their royalty percentages in order to sell *Sandinista!* at half price. After a detour through film—with Jim Jarmusch in particular—and a new start with a bunch of young musicians—Los Mescaleros—Joe Strummer, by dying in 2002, forever made any disappointing reunion impossible.

Drawing on the song on *London Calling*, "Lost in the Supermarket," Olivier Josso pays vibrant tribute to a group that, in addition to making exciting music, were cultural emissaries and raisers of conscience.

LOST in the SUPERMARKET

I've been obsessed with supermarkets since I was 20 years old.

When I was young, I took the "help yourself" sign literally and swiped a load of stuff: records, comic books, candy...

...and the shaving cream I needed for the yearly fights that were part of the Lent festivals.

Careful...

They say some people put razor blades in the plastic of their clubs...

PSSHHH

Shit!

But with the thrill of larceny having passed, supermarkets became literally hostile: it was impossible to go shopping without being overcome by a profound anxiety...

What comes around goes around? No matter what I told myself, I would tremble like a leaf just at the thought of checking out. My head would burn up, I'd break out in an icy cold sweat.

Like the hideous stare of Big Brother, I'd feel the ugliness of consumerism melt over me, a poor worm driven toward omnipotent money, dirty floors, and flourescent lighting.

can...

...can I pay with a check?

In the midst of my torment, I would cling to that song by the Clash, a feverish, rescuing tune that I would hum to myself...

I'm all lost in the supermarket

I can no longer shop happily...

I first heard the Clash in the early 1980s, when I would hunt through Best and Rock & Folk in search of crumbs of information on Kiss and AC/DC.

Transfixed by my obsessions of the moment, I would absent-mindedly absorb the other photographs that filled the pages like subliminal messages...

There was a new program on television: always madly hoping to catch my favorite groups, I'd stay up to ungodly hours watching "Les enfants du rock."

One night they played "Rude Boy"... Half asleep, I heard a jumble of feelings and violent energy, a clash of excitement and disillusion.

Having almost no knowledge of hard rock, it was at that point that I discovered an entirely new universe: along with regular images of the Clash, on stage and at large, there were social battles, street fights and raw visions of a clueless society.

Among the uncertain turmoil of those dirty and explosive times, there was RAY GANGE: co-writer and a central character of the movie. An indecisive figure, he appears to be defined by contradictions, at times annoying, at times endearing.

Hobbling along, I followed his wandering and sway-ing... "Rude Boy"? As early as 1965 in Jamaica, the term was a name for the bad boy associated with rocksteady, the first local underground movement... ☙

It's no coincidence that in my mind, I associate the Clash with the hazy memory of *The Harder They Come*—shown in the same venues as *Rude Boy*, this Jamaican movie tells the story of Ivan, a young singer played by Jimmy Cliff...

... who goes to Kingston to try his luck and—what a paradox—becomes a gunman on the run at the same time that his song becomes a hit throughout the island.

Without changing my musical tastes at the time—hard rock, if you're interested—these two movies echoed my condition at that moment: I was 14 years old and I only hoped to escape the hammer of adulthood, and the anvil of reality.

Like any good rebellious teenager, I rejected everything except my navel and idiotic things.... at Christmas in 1982, a punk friend and I decided to go to the city...

For two straight days, making the most of the wealth of the holidays and our complete recklessness, we got our hands on a gold-mine of vinyl and paper.

For educational purposes, I stole a Pistols album and one by the Exploited, and glanced through my accomplices exotic finds.

A few years later, as the head hard rocker on the bus that took me from the sticks to school, I naturally became friends with the resident punks.

Between pariahs, we helped each other out... although I did think twice when the guy suggested we hold up people at an ATM.

Curious about hearing the Clash on vinyl, I borrowed Sandinista! from a friend... but I wasn't nearly mature enough to grasp its complexity.

Um...

It's a funky mish-mash

hi

ho

ha

Too much, too soon?... Taking a look at what came before my heavy rock friends, I creamed the crop, one step at a time: Alice Cooper, the Dolls, Bowie, and Lou Reed guided me through the bare essentials...

Soon, as I was losing my footing in life, it was the whole skeleton that saved me.

oh boy

I feverishly tracked down rock and roll music, tapping the original sap from the trunks of the mightiest oaks of rock.

Finally, when a dear friend gave me The Clash, I instinctively took to it. London Calling followed suit and immediately entered my daily life.

Police and thieves in the street

With Laure, we decided to share everything. Give 'Em Enough Rope was in his collection and we got hold of Combat Rock right when we started living together.

Somewhere between a Spanish inn and a squat, the building in which we lived was also home to other outcasts. Every day brought parties, weirdos, relationships, addictions... and I liked it.

The eighties were on their last legs and music in the new decade would be a mixed bag: in our attic, in addition to the perennial Cramps, we danced to the Bad Brains, Urban Dance Squad, Run DMC...

Ten years later, the century was coming to a close and life on Earth accelerated—the Clash had broken up a long time ago, but still released a new live album...

Ironically, it was also the first time I couldn't wait for one of their records. In my old fantasy, to be able to go back in time and be at those concerts of the past I dreamed about, the Clash was always at the top of the list...

...and they weren't even my favorite group. That might be what it's all about: the Clash belong to everyone and no one. It's a question of openness, humanity, energy...

They said release "Remote control"

ratapl fratlap

Few groups have been able to unite different tribes so successfully, embody the melting pot without falling into cliché, even in their music!

But we didn't want it on the label

In terms of building bridges, they're kings: how many children for one "Sandinista!"? Yet, on top of the attitude and musical crossbreeding, there's the same feeling of sharing, of collective electric communication, in Massive Attack, Tricky, Asian Dub Foundation, and Le Tigre...

They said "Fly to amsterdam"

...that special feeling, the kind you get at a good party or at a magical concert, when you're vibrating in harmony with others...

Listen to the music!

People laughed but...

God bless rock 'n' roll, the title of Kamel's 2003 brilliant documentary. Starting with Bob Marley's "Johnny Was," covered by Stiff Little Fingers, the Irish punk band, the auteur sheds light on the sources of the phenomenon and makes enlightening connections between its many branches...

Ooh...

With supporting commentary by the eminent Greil Marcus, Kamel draws a parallel between the founding groups of rock and roll and civil rights leaders, both of which came out of the south in the States: Elvis and Martin Luther King, closely related.

Marcus discusses the symbolic name of a doo-wop song by the Nutmegs: "Story untold" (1955). According to him, this unspoken tale contains the fundamental message of original rock and roll...

Life is much more than you think.

There are more people like you than you've been told.

You can experience things they never told you about...

NUTMEGS

With the Clash, these same ideas shine out of an open book on the back of Combat Rock

THE FUTURE IS UNWRITTEN

KNOW YOUR RIGHTS

The explosive connection of all utopias, this is their heart song, which beats in our heads, gets our blood going, and gives us the courage to continue.

Epilogue: And the supermarket?... Now that I have kids, I can get lost there more happily...

no more lost in the supermarket

at last

I can shop

happily

★ Dedicated to the memory of Bo Diddley. ~   Olivier Josso ~

165

Troublemakers—even thugs—chauvinists, opportunists, crooks, etc. In their early years these Englishmen stirred up a lot of animosity and hatred in their wake. But when you choose to call yourself the Stranglers of Guildford (a city in Surrey, southeast of London), aren't you looking to unleash rage and become public enemy number one among rockers? Hugh Cornwell, the charismatic singer, even formed his first band with American military deserters! It didn't take long for the Stranglers to build their reputation as outlaws and journalist-beaters. Times were certainly more rebellious; generations clashed and the nation was not one happy family.

the stranglers

FORMED IN 1974

A story by Serge Clerc

In 1975, when the four-man band (in addition to Cornwell: Jean-Jacques Burnel, whose parents were French, on bass guitar and backup vocals; Jet Black on drums; and Dave Greenfield on the synthesizer) moved to London and played the pub circuit, they had arrived just before the punk revolution, when the youth rose up and revived the English rock scene. Despite their more sophisticated aesthetic (Greenfield's keyboards are reminiscent of Ray Manzarek, the organist for the Doors), they nevertheless rode the punk wave, exploiting it to become more visible and sign a record deal. In 1977, their first album made the charts, coming right after the Damned and the Clash. Some punk purists (early on) said they were jumping on the bandwagon, a criticism based on the fact that the Stranglers knew how to play—being amateur was a supreme virtue at the time—and didn't fit the bill (see the furious look of a Cornwell scorned). But the Stranglers held their own, arguing that today's punks were their fans yesterday. Because of their energy on stage and their aggressive attitude (insults, etc.), they attracted fans of hardcore and hooligans nicknamed the Finchley Boys, who were always ready to deal with other gangs.

The Stranglers were definitely not an empty threat—no one wanted any trouble with Burnel, who had a black belt in karate. Because he tended to see girls in a sexist, bawdy, and ambiguous way—on their first two albums

TROUBLEMAKERS, THUGS, CHAUVINISTS, OPPORTUNISTS, AND CROOKS

you just have to hear 'London Lady,' an attack on a London journalist; or 'Peaches,' with its lascivious thoughts; or 'Bring on the Nubiles,' which starts with "I want to love you like your dad"—the band was singled out by feminists. But instead of playing it down, they chose instead to give a concert in the middle of a London park with stripper friends as guest stars. The difficult year of 1980 didn't slow their momentum. Hugh Cornwell started the year in jail for possession of drugs. Then in the spring, the whole group landed in cells in southern France. During a festival at the University of Nice, the Stranglers concert degenerated because of technical problems; the group was accused of having incited a riot, and wreaked havoc. The following year, in *The Gospel According to the Men in Black*, and in surprising contrast, he revealed his belief in paranormal phenomena and, in a jumble of religious concerns, pointed to those famous men in black who come to visit people who've seen extraterrestrials. Before Hugh Cornwell left the band in August 1990, the group sought success in the United States. They kept the flame alive after his departure with two stand-in singers (Paul Roberts and Baz Warne) and, in 2004, returned to credible roots with the album *Norfolk Coast*. In the pages that follow, Serge Clerc, in the vein of his collaborations with Philippe Manoeuvre on *Métal Hurlant*, stages himself as a rock reporter researching the Stranglers.

THE STRANGLERS! YOU KNOW! THEIR MUSIC BEARS THE INFLUENCE OF DOORS PSYCHEDELICS AND THE STANDELLS!! J.J. BURNEL'S BASS GUITAR IS MONSTROUS! THE LYRICS: FROM THE CHAUVINISM OF "SOMETIMES" TO "DOWN IN THE SEWER", WHICH TALKS ABOUT RAPING A RAT DOWN THERE, HA HA!

THE STRANGLERS POSE AS BASTARDS, THEY GOAD AND PROVOKE!!! HA!

SHIT, YOU'RE STILL HERE?

YEAH, UH, NO!

METAL HURLANT

TYPE TYPE

GET OUT

GET OUT

PHIL MAN

TAKE OFF!

NIiiiAAAON WVRRAOOUM

ENGLAND, LONDON... CHURCHILL, WESTMINSTER, THE NORTHWEST BREEZE, THE THAMES...

ARRIVAL!

WE'VE ARRIVED

GREAT!

SPLASH

CARNABY STREET. THE N.M.E. OFFICES, NEIL SPENCER, THE EDITOR IN CHIEF...

...HULLO, I'M HERE FROM FRANCE, PHIL MAN SENT ME!

N.M.E

SO I HANDED IN MY FIRST INTERNATIONAL DRAWING!

1979... AT THAT TIME THERE WERE EDITORIAL MEETINGS AT METAL HURLANT

FOR THE NEXT ISSUE, I WANT 10 PAGES

ME, TOO!

WHAT VIOLENCE. AAH...

CALM DOWN NOW

OUCH! I WANT

ASS HOLE!!

ACTUALLY... UM, WELL YES... SURE, I'LL DO A COMIC STRIP ON THE STRANGLERS! SOMETHING PRETTY LONG... LIKE, UM... 40 PAGES!!!

NME

METAL

...?

40 PAGES... UM, YEAH, WE'LL SEE!!

SOUTHERN COMFORT

FEEL LIKE A WOG

NEW WAVE BY

I DELVED INTO MY REVIEWS.

BUT I'VE NEVER SEEN A MORE IMPRESSIVE GROUP THAN THE HEARTBREAKERS THAT NIGHT AT THE VORTEX IN LONDON... AND OF COURSE ROCK HAS BECOME DANGEROUS!

PHIL MAN **CHEAP THRILLS** SPECIALS, LET'S DANCE THE POGO!!

A GREAT DANCE! JUMP IN THE AIR, THEN THE FUN STARTS— HURL YOURSELF INTO THE GUY NEXT TO YOU AND KNOCK HIM OVER. YOU'LL KNOCK EVERYONE OVER AND IT'S REALLY COOL!! WHEN YOU FALL, MAKE SURE YOU BITE THE GUY NEXT TO YOU.

Rock & fol

TIMES WERE ABOUT VIOLENCE, TIMES WERE ALL ABOUT BEING PUNK!

PUNK BAD BOYS... the STRANGLERS

BRING ON the NUBILES!

SUCK

I TOOK LOTS OF NOTES.

1977 IN PARIS, J.J. BURNEL KNOCKED OUT A YANKEE, VISIBLY HIGH ON AMYL-NITRATES, WHO WANTED TO USE HIM AS A BUMPER ON HIS CADILLAC. J.J. BURNEL, AN ADMIRER OF MISHIMA (THE JAPANESE NATIONALIST POET WHO COMMITTED SUICIDE) IS A BLACK BELT IN KARATE...

I WAS GATHERING ARTICLES AND WAS COUNTING ON STEALING BITS. AFTER ALL SHAKESPEARE MUST HAVE WORKED LIKE THAT, TAKING THIS AND THAT... THEN ADDING HIS OWN TOUCH. IT WORKED FOR HIM. YOU'VE GOT TO KNOW HOW TO STEAL!

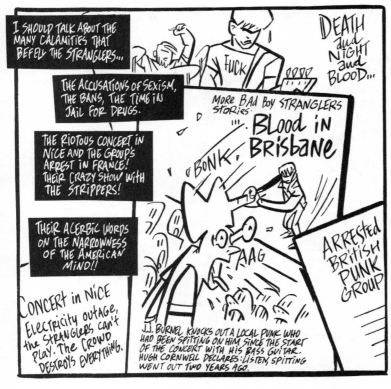

I SHOULD TALK ABOUT THE MANY CALAMITIES THAT BEFELL THE STRANGLERS...

THE ACCUSATIONS OF SEXISM, THE BANS, THE TIME IN JAIL FOR DRUGS.

THE RIOTOUS CONCERT IN NICE AND THE GROUP'S ARREST IN FRANCE! THEIR CRAZY SHOW WITH THE STRIPPERS!

THEIR ACERBIC WORDS ON THE NARROWNESS OF THE AMERICAN MIND!!

CONCERT IN NICE. ELECTRICITY OUTAGE, THE STRANGLERS CAN'T PLAY. THE CROWD DESTROYS EVERYTHING.

FUCK

DEATH and NIGHT and BLOOD...

MORE BAD BOY STRANGLERS STORIES... **Blood in Brisbane**

BONK

AAG

ARRESTED BRITISH PUNK GROUP

J.J. BURNEL KNOCKS OUT A LOCAL PUNK WHO HAD BEEN SPITTING ON HIM SINCE THE START OF THE CONCERT WITH HIS BASS GUITAR. HUGH CORNWELL DECLARES: LISTEN, SPITTING WENT OUT TWO YEARS AGO.

AAAAA! THE PUNK JOURNEY!!! I LOVE THOSE SHORT PERIODS IN HISTORY WHEN TIME SEEMS TO ACCELERATE... LIKE "THE FRENCH REVOLUTION," 2 MINUTES AGO, YOU WERE IN GREAT SHAPE; 2 MINUTES LATER, THEY'VE CHOPPED OFF YOUR HEAD!!!

I WANT 80 PAGES!

YEAH, YEAH...

172

173

The incredible destiny of a few ordinary kids from the north of England: Bernard Sumner, Peter Hook, and Stephen Morris. In three intense years, with Joy Division, they composed a soundtrack for their oppressive times (thanks to Thatcher), when the hopes of English youth were crushed. Then they buried Ian Curtis, their hypnotic singer, and reinvented themselves, igniting with New Order the romance between rock and electric dance music. First they changed their city, Manchester; then the world and the spirit of rockers, pushing them out onto the dance floor and coaxing them out of their clumsiness. Not bad for this group of lively, unpretentious bandmates, who admitted, twenty years into their career, that it was better to be dead drunk after a concert than before.

You had to be from Manchester, that grim and polluted industrial city, to call your band Joy Division—named for that contingent of women the Nazis forced to be prostitutes in order to raise morale among German soldiers. Especially considering that the same band was originally named Warsaw, paying homage to a Bowie instrumental song ("Warszawa" on *Low*), but also invoking the biggest Jewish ghetto during the Second World War. Nevertheless, the controversy arising from such dark fascinations was overcome in the first months of Joy Division's existence by the strangeness of the group and its singer. Enthralled by psychological disorders and human suffering, Ian Curtis succumbed to epileptic fits, sometimes on stage. In his very austere lyrics, failure, darkness, and distance form a bleak and contagious poetry to which his baritone voice, similar to Jim Morrison's of the Doors, added a dramatic dimension.

Emerging while the flames of punk were still burning, Joy Division quickly aligned themselves with the cold sound of the Cure and became the symbol of the English label Factory Records, a true laboratory founded by Tony Wilson, espousing a strong and independent aesthetic (see *24-Hour Party People*, a film by Michael Winterbottom). The meticulous producer Martin Hannett, who in particular requested that Stephen Morris pare down his drumming to the bare minimum,

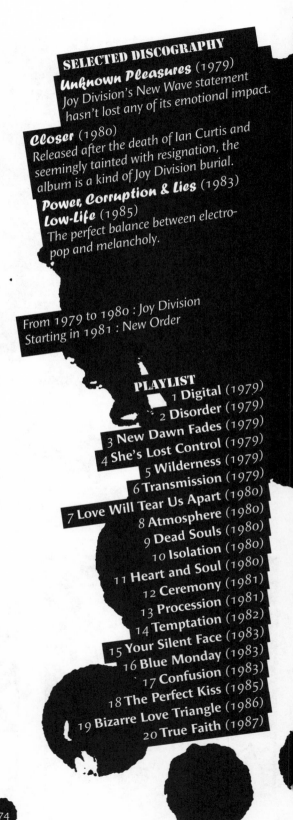

SELECTED DISCOGRAPHY

Unknown Pleasures (1979)
Joy Division's New Wave statement hasn't lost any of its emotional impact.

Closer (1980)
Released after the death of Ian Curtis and seemingly tainted with resignation, the album is a kind of Joy Division burial.

Power, Corruption & Lies (1983)

Low-Life (1985)
The perfect balance between electro-pop and melancholy.

From 1979 to 1980 : Joy Division
Starting in 1981 : New Order

PLAYLIST
1 Digital (1979)
2 Disorder (1979)
3 New Dawn Fades (1979)
4 She's Lost Control (1979)
5 Wilderness (1979)
6 Transmission (1979)
7 Love Will Tear Us Apart (1980)
8 Atmosphere (1980)
9 Dead Souls (1980)
10 Isolation (1980)
11 Heart and Soul (1980)
12 Ceremony (1981)
13 Procession (1981)
14 Temptation (1982)
15 Your Silent Face (1983)
16 Blue Monday (1983)
17 Confusion (1983)
18 The Perfect Kiss (1985)
19 Bizarre Love Triangle (1986)
20 True Faith (1987)

A
story by
Nylso

FIRST, THEY CHANGED THEIR CITY, MANCHESTER; THEN THE WORLD AND THE SPIRIT OF ROCKERS, PUSHING THEM OUT ONTO THE DANCE FLOOR

accentuated the uniqueness of Joy Division and its icy world, where Peter Hook's bass also played a prominent role. Before the second album *Closer* was released, Curtis, weakened from tranquilizers and prone to guilt because he was pulled between his wife and a mistress, let depression get the best of him (see *Control*, the movie by Anton Corbijn). In May 1980, on the eve of Joy Division's first American tour, he hanged himself. He was 23 years old. The three others decided to continue under the equally loaded name New Order. After mourning musically, Bernard Sumner took over at the mic and gave the keyboard (he also played the guitar) over to Gillian Gilbert. Together, they opted to go in an electropop direction that was at times melancholic, but which was clearer. Inspired by their nights in New York clubs, they helped back the opening of the Hacienda, the legendary Manchester venue associated with the rise of house. They didn't stop there, trying through

their own means to tame the technology of the time, beatboxes and the first samplers. One of their attempts resulted in a happy accident, "Blue Monday." Recycling Sylvester's disco or Giorgio Moroder's orgasmic productions for Donna Summer, this song became the biggest selling 12" single of all time. By the late 1980s, under the stupefying influence of ecstasy, Manchester became Madchester. All the young groups, from the Stone Roses to Happy Mondays, added dance to their songs, and New Order became the godfathers of a movement that even made an impression on the Scots in Primal Scream. Since then, the group has toned it down to the point of (almost) not existing. But the mix of pop and electro continues to be a reference for musicians, such as Moby, Franz Ferdinand, and the Chemical Brothers. Not bad for a few ordinary kids from the north of England . . . Nylso takes a look at what they stirred in him.

NEW ORDER

I like cemeteries
and New Order

And Chopin.

The ethereal contours of leaves can show us temples, forests, and storms.

Like the cover of Joy Division's *Closer.*

-CLOSER-

Like the lamentation at the church in Semur-en-Auxois.

"Books descend from books as families descend from families. They resemble their parents, as human children resemble their parents; yet they differ as children differ;

and revolt as children revolt," says Virginia Woolf.

New order, the child of Joy Division

It's really pointless to make a comic strip about a musical subject...

To rehash the same ideas, to talk about the tones of punk, rock, pop...

Low-life

Love vigilantes
The perfect kiss
This time of night
Sunrise
Elegia
Sooner than you think
Sub-culture
Face up

and maybe above all
New ORDER's first album

Joy Division
"CLOSER" first, but
maybe above
all "Still"

THORENS
TD 166 MKII

we can skip the
new titles

Except for
"Republic," but
that's because
I'm a fan

When I was in college, they said I was depressed

Because I listened to Joy Division

And because I liked cemeteries.

I like to be alone.

Like anyone who's hyperactive

I like it when my personal rhythm lowers

in intensity

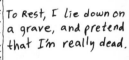

To Rest, I lie down on a grave, and pretend that I'm really dead.

And I observe

Listen and

fall asleep

Among the cats.

JOY DIVISION

It's easy to picture him with "Love" and "Hate" written on his knuckles, like the disturbing religious fanatic Robert Mitchum played in *The Night of the Hunter*. For the great Australian, gentleness and rage are inseparable, like gods and demons, punk rock and gospel. As if he wanted his one voice to have the passion of a romantic crooner like Roy Orbison (the bespectacled 1960s master of vibrato) and the deep and more frightening timbre of Johnny Cash. Nick Cave, with a solid literary education behind him, likes dramatic atmospheres and metaphors. When he launches into ballads, they often smell like sulfur, sometimes worse. Immerse yourself in the duet "Where the Wild Roses Grow," which he sings with his compatriot Kyle Minogue, and you'll feel just how much the joy of life and the dangers of death are interlaced in his work. Despite its calm surface, the song isn't sentimental: it celebrates a love where a passion for beauty dooms a beautiful woman, who is killed by her lover. Haunted by heavenly and horrible creatures, donkeys who see angels and criminals without remorse, both frightening and romantic characters, Nick Cave's world is always about the balance between redemption and perdition. In movies, he could play a psychopath at a high-security prison (*Ghosts of the Civil Dead*, for which he co-wrote the script) or a saloon singer mocking the man who shot Jesse James in the back (*The Assassination of Jesse James by the Coward Robert Ford*).

FOR THE GREAT AUSTRALIAN, GENTLENESS AND RAGE ARE INSEPARABLE, LIKE GODS AND DEMONS, PUNK ROCK AND GOSPEL

POW
POW
POW

NICK CAVE

A story by Laure Del Pino

BORN IN 1957

SELECTED DISCOGRAPHY

From Her to Eternity (1984)
Combines the abrasive post-punk of the
Birthday Party with a darker atmosphere.

Tender Prey (1988)
A turning point and the Cave fan's bible.

Let Love In (1994)
After softer albums, this one
marks a return to fiery rock.

Murder Ballads (1996)
Delicious, somber ballads with Kylie
Minogue, PJ Harvey, and Shane McGowan.

Abattoir Blues/The Lyre of Orpheus (2004)
Blixa Bargeld's leaving coincided with a burst of
energy. A balanced double album.

Nick Cave takes no sides. He explores the human soul, going from traditional blues to the electric fury of rock. Although the Birthday Party, his first group, came into being after punk, and beat the drum for abrasive electric rock, Cave already proved to be less responsive to the nihilism of the Sex Pistols than to the imagination of bluesmen like Leadbelly or John Lee Hooker. A song by the latter, "I'm Gonna Kill That Woman," strongly influenced his writing; he borrowed it for *Kicking Against the Pricks*, an edifying album of covers. Ever since his childhood in Australia, amid a family of practicing Anglicans, he has staked his own territory, a kind of enclave where the depths of religious America, the one depicted in Grant Wood's *American Gothic* (portraying an ambiguous couple, farmers, in front of their gothic-style house), mingles with post-war Berlin. He even starred in Wim Wenders' *Wings of Desire*, in which an angel wanders among humans in the German capital. One of his most talented colleagues was from Berlin, the agitator Blixa Bargeld, the brains behind the dynamic sounds of Einstürzende Neubauten and an apostle of industrial music. But Cave always returns to the blues, forever delivering his own burning incarnation, respecting old forms while modernizing them. It makes sense, because for him, everything converges there: "sex, death, joy, politics, religion . . ." Like Neil Young, the Canadian rocker who's longevity should serve as a model to Cave, the Australian has worked in recent years with both feather and whip, producing collections of peaceful ballads before mounting his electric warhorse again. The violinist Warren Ellis, his most recent right-hand man, has spurred him on, motivating Cave enough to form their side project Grinderman. Laure Del Pino tenderly looks at all these transformations, starting with capillary ones.

The king ink

Nick Cave's career of characters started neither in 2008 with the lively era of "Dig!!! Lazarus Dig!!!", with the the Fu Manchu mustache,

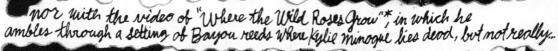

nor with the video of "Where the Wild Roses Grow"*, in which he ambles through a setting of Bayou reeds where Kylie Minogue lies dead, but not really...

*Album: "Murder Ballads"

In reality, it's been more than thirty years that this Australian fetishist has been happily clouding issues. Like the image-fixations he's been collecting naughtilly along the way.

Also, with his first group, as early as 1977: The Boys Next Door (the same as The Birthday Party but before)*, he developed a pantomime act in a New-Wave vein. The song "Shiver" is an example.

BUT MY BABY'S SO VAIN SHE IS ALMOST A MIRROR AND THE SOUND OF

YA YA YA YA YA YA

HER NAME SENDS A NERVOUS SHIVER DOWN MY SPINE DOWN MY SPI YAYAYA YAYAYAYAYAYA YAYAIINNE

Then, fueled by the post-punk reorganization of the Birthday Party, for "Nick the Stripper"² he pranced around in a devilish loin-cloth in a vestal video in decay.

Albums:
1= "Door, Door"
2= "Prayers on Fire"

*First Band (except N.C.): Mick Harvey, Tracy Pew and Phill Calvert. Rowland S. Howard joined the group in 1978.

185

Honey Honey Honey Honey Honey Honey Kiss Me yey!

Yack Yack

In the early 1980s, even if he struggled to rid himself of his image as someone who wanted to release bats under skirts, he came to look more like a king of scrap, a pillar of oddities, with his friend and boss guitarist at his side, Tracy Pew.*

yack Yack Yack

And our cheery fellow even cultivated the grotesque with his hair experiments. Aside from an addiction to black dye,

Berlin period "From Her To Eternity," 1984

Pompadour-Elvis Period, "Kicking Against the Pricks", 1986

"Henry's Dream" Period, Sao Paulo 1992

One will note several distinct phases and stages, both in terms of volume and movement (a few examples above...)

ME

*Highly recommended: "Live 1981-83" released in 1999 on 4AD.

Copy of a drawing by Nick Cave

Nevertheless, no matter what state his hair was in, his sex appeal seemed to work. As proof, check out what Olivier once saw→ According to him, Nick Cave's hair was particularly bad that night.

The guy was so obsessed with the stage that he needed it: "I just feel very comfortable up there in a way that I don't feel off stage. I don't feel that I really fulfill people's expectations of me off stage, but when I'm on stage I do."

Now I'm remembering a crazy concert at the Paris Olympia in 1990, where I was fascinated by his powerful energy. I knew the songs already, but seeing him there, in the flesh, so excited and sweaty... it made him oddly familiar, funny and generous; a bit like an old uncle clowning around.

Offstage, writing is the other need, the mission. "Words influence music." And Nick Cave has been dealing with the same obsessions since the beginning: ambivalence, good vs. evil, chaos, crime, violence, death, faith, bible, and clichéd women, "whores with hearts of gold" or "angelic little girls".

The influence of southern and Shakespearean literature is easy to see.

wild world

During a trip to London with Olivier in August 1989, we went to a Hypnotics and Fuzztones concert at the Electric Ballroom. Then (really) the next day, in the neighborhood, we came across a bookstore ad announcing that Nick Cave would be doing a book signing that day for his novel, And the Ass Saw the Angel. We couldn't have asked for more.

oho ooh ooh like you so...ooh...

so?

THE Book

In front of a orderly line of diverse people, Cave clones included, he looked as lost and alone as Euchrid Euchrow, the hero in the book. We took pictures. But when we got back, we were devastated to find that the roll was blank, probably because it wasn't put in right.

? ?

While he belatedly dragged around his reputation as a poisonous preacher, with a syringe close at hand and hitting the occasional flat note (certain live recordings from the dark period between 1986 and 1988 when he survived several ODs are examples), our Nick had it in his head that he wanted to write a beautiful love song.

THE LOVE SONG

« En français: "Et l'âne vit l'ange" »

Haunted by the influences of: Leonard Cohen, Elvis Presley, Suicide, Johnny Cash, The Stooges, John Lee Hooker, Einstürzende Neubauten... he transcended and soulfully moved on.

In fact, the first albums with the Bad Seeds* have a captivating and heartrending depth. Songs like "A box for Black Paul" will leave you speechless. You see that Nick Cave can reinvent the blues...

*The Pillars (except N.C): Mick Harvey, Blixa Bargeld and Thomas Wydler.

#"From Her to Eternity"

...and can master the cover, like on "Kicking Against the Pricks."

Except that, by singing too many love songs and running after fame, he ended up growing weary. Since the early 1990s, his six or so albums will make you yawn, except for "Murder Ballads".

He seems to make fun of himself more and more as time goes on. And yet, isn't he always looking to hide his lovelorn heart behind his shades and Lee Hazelwood mustache? You have to see him shed a tear during a 1987 concert singing "500 Miles". He cries like a fallen emperor... caught up in his feelings about being away from home for so long.

METALLICA

FORMED IN 1981

FUUUCK
FUCK OFF
SHIIIT
FUCK

A story by Riad Sattouf

Faster, higher, louder. To rival their peers—other groups who had upped the decibel and noise levels—Metallica adopted an Olympic credo, mixing it with the mentality of the 300 Spartan warriors. When the group entered the arena in 1982 with their front man, the singer-guitarist James Hetfield, looking like a Viking, it meant that a battle of electric gladiators was about to begin. Their elders were those bands that teenagers played to rebel against and enrage their parents. Before Metallica, there were the unleashed Australians AC/DC and their hard, burning blues, which represented wild rock on the loose; but there was also the slovenly English band, Motörhead, who also spread the good word—specifically: "If it's too loud, it's because you're too old." As knights in service of the cause, Metallica regularly bowed before the group led by the mustachioed icon Lemmy, even naming a song after him,

"Motorbreath." Stirred also by the showy heavy metal of Iron Maiden and the hardcore punk of the Misfits, the group that formed around the Hetfield-Ulrich backbone (Lars Ulrich, the drummer and backup vocalist) surpassed its competition by dramatically speeding up metal. Their first albums, fueled by adrenaline, made a name for thrash, a speedier and more brutal version of metal.

In the 1980s, while a wave of hard rockers in makeup, spandex tights, and bandanas flirted with ballads on FM radio, Metallica set fires alight with other outsiders, challenging the ridiculous decorum of Bon Jovi and their cohorts in the name of a pure, hard attitude—James Hetfield even carved "kill Bon Jovi" into his guitar. Coming onstage to the soundtrack of *The Good, The Bad and The Ugly*, the four-man band assailed any traitors who watered down their metal.

But they also attacked existential anxieties that burdened the morale and soul of sympathetic warriors: the attraction of power, the fear of waning rage. Inspired by the science-fiction writer H. P. Lovecraft (one of their songs is called "The Call of Ktulu"), the members of the group fought continually against disaster. First, their tendency to live life to the fullest. Like barbaric hedonists, the band members indulged too heartily in excess, earning the nickname "Alcoholica." One day, while he was telling off Hetfield, scolding him like a child for the damage he caused at one of the venues, the American promoter Bill Graham told him he had had the same conversation with Sid Vicious, the daredevil bassist of the Sex Pistols, and Keith Moon, the drummer and reveler of the Who—both dead. As their success grew worldwide, the brutes of Metallica proved to be vulnerable—the accidental death of the legendary bassist Cliff Burton in 1986 remains an unhealed wound. Even the discreet Kirk Hammett,

a guitarist whose playing was as wild as his hair, admitted that metal was a form of therapy for him, especially since he had been abused as a child by his neighbor. The distress deepened when bassist Jason Newsted (who replaced Burton) left in 2001. In-fighting, Hetfield's alcoholism, and even the disenchantment of fans after the band sued Napster (the online music sharing service) inspired them to a hire a pricey therapist so that Metallica could combat the monster it had become (see the staggering documentary *Some Kind of Monster*). Since then, the band have rediscovered their rage—and also recovered their status as setters of metal standards, still revered by fans like Riad Sattouf.

THEIR FIRST ALBUMS, FUELED BY ADRENALINE, MADE A NAME FOR THRASH, A SPEEDIER AND MORE BRUTAL VERSION OF METAL

SELECTED DISCOGRAPHY

Kill 'em All (1983)
Never missing a beat, this bloody, thrash metal doesn't quit.

Ride the Lightning (1984)
Slightly more sophisticated than its predecessor, but just as powerful.

Masters of Puppets (1986)
The classic album of Metallica's first period and the last record to include Cliff Burton, the genius bassist.

Metallica (1991)
Referred to as the "black album" because of its cover, the songs are more considered and direct. The group gains mass appeal.

PLAYLIST

1 **The Four Horsemen** (1983)
2 **Motorbreath** (1983)
3 **Seek and Destroy** (1983)
4 **Fight Fire with Fire** (1984)
5 **For Whom the Bell Tolls** (1984)
6 **Fade to Black** (1984)
7 **Battery** (1986)
8 **Master of Puppets** (1986)
9 **Welcome Home** (1986)
10 **Blackened** (1988)
11 **One** (1988)
12 **Harvester of Sorrow** (1988)
13 **Enter Sandman** (1991)
14 **The Unforgiven** (1991)
15 **Wherever I May Roam** (1991)
16 **Nothing Else Matters** (1991)
17 **Hero of the Day** (1996)
18 **The Memory Remains** (1997)
19 **Frantic** (2005)
20 **All Within My Hands** (2005)

THE MEMBERS OF
METALLICA

AND A FEW FACTS ABOUT THEIR LIFE

JAMES HETFIELD is the singer and rhythm guitarist. He's the bandleader (with LARS)

In the beginning, james had a certain look and a way about him. We knew he would have been our friend if he were in our class.

1984

FUUUCK
FUCK OFF
SHiiiT
FUCK

during concerts, it's like he has Tourettes. It's like he's cursing life for having given him so much success.

1997

BURP

james became an alcoholic because he was a normal guy who skyrocketed to success.

he loves harleys and tuning up cars.

When he plays, he looks like he's masturbating.

AHAHAAH MAAAN
FUCK
HAHA
FUCK YA
HAA
SHiT

james, cracking up after someone joked about the smell of his farts.

The evolution of James Hetfield's face since the beginning of Metallica.

1983   1990   1992   1997   2009

1

LARS ULRICH is the drummer and one of the founders with james. He's Danish and the son of a tennis pro.

he bangs the drums as if he were beating a dog nibbling at his balls.

1984

he's a big fan of modern art and is a double-pedal god.

Despite his puny, average physique, he acts like he's a top model. He inspires confidence among the ugly.

he always wears glasses that are too big for him.

The evolution of Lors' face:

1983   1997   2000   2009

LARS ULRICH meets his wife (true story)

In a bar, in the 1990s...

Good evening, can i buy you a drink?

um, no, who are you?

my name is LARS ULRICH and i'm an international rock star.

Then they go get married.

2

KIRK HAMMETT is the lead guitarist, which means he plays all the solos.

A sad, sensitive look

he's very effeminate and really skinny.

when he was young, he took guitar lessons with JOE SATRIANI.

ONE MORE TIME

Wait, I've got to rest my hand. It hurts.

He had lots of silky hair, like a mane, but he ended up cutting it, too.

Kirk is very lovable. He's very quiet and obeys James and Lars. He often wears sunglasses that are too big for him. One day, he declared:

The thing I like most in life is not playing the guitar...

... or being on stage...

... it's reading comics in bed.

he got married

he owns huge Percheron horses that he rides whenever he can.

a horse similar to the horse in DEATH DEALER, Frank Frazetta's famous painting.

he was a drunk and got thrown out.

KIRK NOW

Dave Mustaine, the brilliant founder of Megadeth, was Metallica's first lead guitarist.

3

Metallica has had several bassists. the first and best one was **CLIFF BURTON**.

He had the face of a teenager.

he was a genius bass player. They say his songwriting was influenced by Bach.

he was the first metal guy to do bass solos.

Unfortunately, Cliff was run over by a bus after a concert and died.

he was replaced by **JASON NEWSTED** a pretty grim guy.

After a while, jason got fed up and left metallica. the group became depressed and was on the verge of exploding.

he wore bellbottoms but was a sick headbanger.

Robert Trujillo took over.
He's the best bassist metal has.

Every member of metallica eventually cut his hair, but Robert has always kept his long. He's so cool.

Robert Trujillo and his famous live playing

he's a surfer →

it's touching the ground!

he looks like a cave man. you've got to see it to believe it.

Robert wears sunglasses that fit.

Riad Sattouf

4

195

A
story by
Jochen Gerner

Pixies

FORMED IN 1986

While every group relies on the chemistry that bonds its members, the kind that existed between the four Pixies had the intensity of a shooting star, blinding but brief. Although the group artificially extended its life by getting back together in 2004, it ran its course in a very short time span (1986–1991). During these five short years, the quartet that was Charles Thompson a.k.a. Black Francis (vocals and guitar), Kim Deal (bass), Joey Santiago (guitar), and Divide Lovering (drums) launched into the unknown with a thousand dollars borrowed from Francis's father and forever transformed American rock.

Playing the anti-glamour card (no look, Francis's belly, and an austere stage presence) the Pixies never really had their feet firmly on the ground. In order to recruit a (female) bassist, Black Francis and Joey Santiago—an inimitable guitarist fluctuating between punk and flamenco—published a small ad in which they described the idea for the sound of their future group, hoping to straddle Hüsker Dü, the reputed hardcore punk band, and Peter, Paul & Mary, the nicest and most popular folk band of the 1960s.

Recycled soon afterward (with greater success) by Nirvana, the contrast between soft melody and violence, lulls and bursts, became the backbone of the Pixies repertoire. Black Francis—who would write his songs standing in front of the mirror so that he could find the rocker moves he dreamed about as a kid—invented unusual combinations of the Beatles and Iggy Pop, surf music and Elvis Costello. Not only did this prolific songwriter end up gradually suffocating the otherwise talented Kim Deal, but he also imposed his imagination on the others, an imagination fed by the deviance of science fiction and an attraction to the dreamlike strangeness and perversity of David Lynch.

Drawn to the craft of the 1960s, Francis would have liked to travel back to a time when MTV didn't exist, when rock was still an underground culture. In their four albums—each with a cover designed by Vaughan Oliver, who would emphasize their uniqueness—the singer introduced bizarre ideas inspired by events like the supposed visit of an alien to Roswell, New Mexico, in 1947. Characters taken from the Bible, borrowed from numerology, or

in homage to Gustave Eiffel also inspired him and became part of the group's lyrical museum. Jochen Gerner provides an almost exhaustive review in the pages that follow.

Black Francis—who swears that as a child he saw a flying saucer land on top of his parent's house—has always fantasized about being the first musician to play on the moon. Obsessed with space and travel—he has used some of his earnings to make his dreams come true: a cruise and a flight on the

WHILE EVERY GROUP RELIES ON THE CHEMISTRY THAT BONDS ITS MEMBERS, THE KIND THAT EXISTED BETWEEN THE FOUR PIXIES HAD THE INTENSITY OF A SHOOTING STAR, BLINDING BUT BRIEF.

Concorde, the supersonic airliner—he became convinced that he had to escape alone for his career to take off. After the last album, *Trompe le Monde*, on which he used the others to interpret his ideas, he unilaterally decided to fly off on his own. Unfortunately for him, without Joey Santiago's guitar and Kim Deal's voice, his songs no longer had the same strange charm, that unstable balance of pop and noise. Even though he composed with the same appetite as before, tinkering with country, soul, and folk, he had to give up on his ambitions. And it was Kim Deal and her Breeders, a group they formed for fun, that enjoyed a return to grace and success with "Cannonball." With its memorable bass line, the song became one of the hits of the grunge years, along with "Smells Like Teen Spirit." Later, admired by Kurt Cobain, Thom Yorke of Radiohead, Damon Albarn of Blur and . . . David Bowie, who covered one of their songs, the Pixies were revived and pocketed the benefits of being a cult favorite.

PIXIES RAW MATERIALS

DIRTY FLOOR

SALTY WINE

WATER

ICE

CACTUS TREE

OIL IN THE CHAIN

CEMENT FLOOR

BURIED WEST

DIAMOND

TEN MILLION POUNDS OF SLUDGE

PRETTY THING

FIRE BREATHING

GOOD ROPE

SILVER

FOREVERGREEN

BIG BIG STONE

VELVETEEN

SHINE OF THE EVER

LITTLE THINGS

DIFFERENT GROUND

VELOURIA

FIRE

SALT LAKE

RAIN

WARM NIGHT

FISSION

TALENTED WINE

SMOKE

FLUID NAMED EXTINCTION

WOODY EAST

CLASSICAL GAS

REFLECTIONS

BRINE

JELLYROLL

BREAD

AIR

BAD SHOES

GRASS

MARIJUANA

DRY CANALS

SOUP

WIND

WALLS

PILLARS

198

PIXIES DEEPEST SPACE

GOD IS SEVEN

GOD IN THE SKY

HEAVEN

Heaven

MONKEY

CUPIDS AND ANGELS

HOLE IN THE SKY

TOP OF THE SKY

CREATURE

DARK

NO ATMOSPHERE

WHEN THE PLANET HIT THE SUN

SOME SUN

ONLY SPACE

PLANET OF GLASS

S

BAKING IN THE SUN

BURNING IN DEEPEST SPACE

STARS

MARTIAN HONEY

6

DEVIL IS SIX

PLANET OF SOUND

UNDRESSING IN THE SUN

YOU GROPE FOR LUNA

ME FLYING IN THE AIR

SKYWALK

WHITE MOON'S HOT

SKY

NIGHT

STARRY SKY

SUN SHINES IN THE RUSTY MORNING

BENEATH THE SKY

SNOW

UTAH

MOUNTAINS

SUNLIGHT INTO THE MOUNTAIN

UNIVERSITY OF MASSACHUSETTS

SKYLINE OF THE OLYMPUS MONS

SWIMMIN' IN THE CARIBBEAN

DESERT HEAT

PALACE OF THE BRINE

5

MAN IS FIVE

THE FRAYED COLOR OF ICE

WAY OUT IN THE WATER

RIVER EUPHRATES

LAKE

LAKE LIKE OCEAN

FLOATING IN THE WATER

DEAD SEA

STINKING ISLAND

AN UNDER WATER GUY WHO CONTROLLED THE SEA.

DRIVE MY CAR INTO THE OCEAN

NEPTUNE'S ONLY DAUGHTER

LISTEN TO THE SEA

ACROSS THE OCEAN SAILING

RETURN TO SEA-BYE

PIXIES ANATOMY

PIXIES WILD ANIMALS

BEANS AND HORSES LARD

ANIMALS WERE HIDING BEHIND THE ROCK EXCEPT THE LITTLE FISH.

RIDE AROUND MY BICYCLE LIKE A PONY

LA VIDA TOTAL ES UN PORQUERIA

NUESTRO PROPRIO ANIMAL

CHIEN ANDALUSIA

3X

CARIBOU

CRUSTACEANS

MONKEY

MERMAID

PIG

A PLAIN WITH NO HERD

LEMUR

A PET AT MY SIDE

NOT EVEN A BIRD

SEA-MONKEY

EROTIC VULTURE

APRIL BIRDS

FISH

EXTRA-TERRESTRIALS

VAMPIRE

BIRD

SIREN

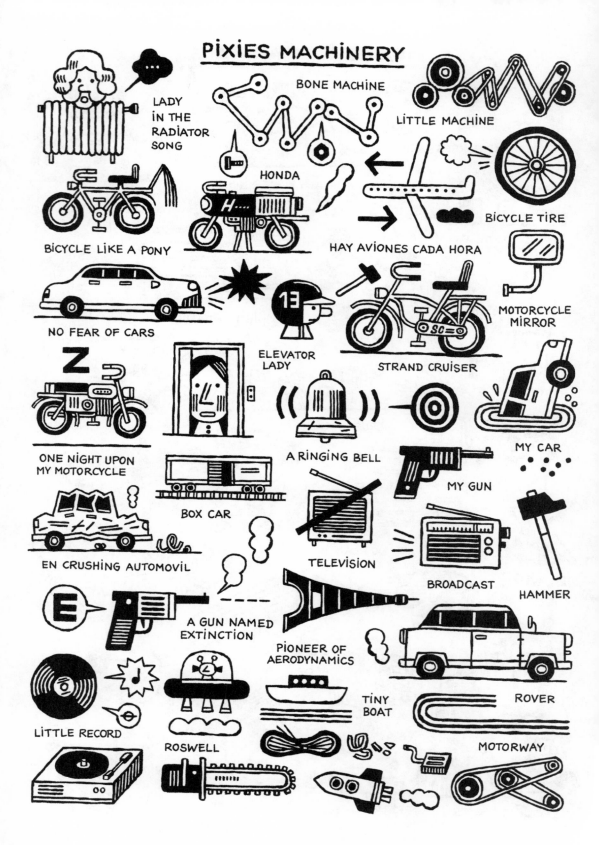

PiXIES MACHINERY

LADY iN THE RADIATOR SONG

BONE MACHINE

LITTLE MACHINE

HONDA

BiCYCLE LIKE A PONY

HAY AVIONES CADA HORA

BiCYCLE TIRE

NO FEAR OF CARS

ELEVATOR LADY

STRAND CRUISER

MOTORCYCLE MIRROR

ONE NIGHT UPON MY MOTORCYCLE

A RINGING BELL

MY GUN

MY CAR

BOX CAR

TELEVISION

BROADCAST

HAMMER

EN CRUSHING AUTOMOVIL

A GUN NAMED EXTINCTION

PiONEER OF AERODYNAMICS

LITTLE RECORD

ROSWELL

TINY BOAT

ROVER

MOTORWAY

PIXIES ONOMATOPOEIA

UH-OH, UH-OH, UH-OH, UH-OH

YEP, YEP YEP YEP !

UH-HU, UH-HU, UH-HU, UH-HU, OOO

OOOOOOH-STOP

OOOOH OOOOH

WAVIN HI HI HI HI HI

OOOOH

OH MY GOLLY ! OH MY GOLLY !

G-G-G-GIMME

HUH ?

ROSA, OH OH OOH ROSA !

HUH HUH

HHHH

CARIBOUUUUU

RE-PE-ENT

LAAAA LAAA PATRIA

OH OH OH OH OH

UH

NO, NO, NO, NO, NOOO

HA-HAAA

OH BURY ME

HA-HA HA-HA

AAAHH

HA HA HA HO

UH HUH HUH

TAAAMME

HH-HH

HEY

CRACK CRACK CRACKITY JONES

YEAH

OH NEPTUNE

LA LA LA LA LA LA LA LA

HUH ?

LA LA LOVE YOU

HEY

OH WELL

HOOOOOOH

YOO HOO

UH

HI !

UH

SKYYYYYYY

WAAAOH

D = R × T

OH

OH OH

JOCHEN GERNER

"I'm a creep, I'm a weirdo/What the hell am I doing here?" That a song about self-hatred and distress like "Creep" launched Radiohead's career is significant, because the group's story has been so influenced by discomfort, distrust of fame and material things—usually the stuff of being a rock star. For example, some fifteen years after "Creep," these Oxfordians refused to reveal the sum they earned by releasing *In Rainbows* on the Internet for free, letting crazy rumors spread rather than clearing up the mystery. Except for when they do concerts, they've preferred to turn inward. All of Radiohead's ambiguity is embodied in their singer and thinking soul, Thom Yorke. At once ambitious and self-conscious, he has become a pop star despite his frail body and strange face, distinguished by a partially shut eyelid (resulting from an operation on his left eye). Yorke's anticonformist and unpredictable charisma nevertheless made him one of the figureheads of the 1990s, someone whose melancholy verges on bliss, as in Morgan Navarro's story. The fact that the group refused to play the game of a public life and went around the rules of the music industry has never affected their influence. Radiohead wouldn't exist without Yorke's moving voice, a unique *falsetto*, and his melancholy. But, alone, he wouldn't have been able to trigger and manage the revolution that the quintet's pyramid-shaped discography represents—the rough base that was the first and clumsy album released during the grunge wave, with later albums becoming more and more elegant. Yorke had to wait for his friends, Ed O'Brien (guitar), Phil Selway (drums), and the Greenwood brothers (Colin on bass guitar and Jonny on lead guitar), to finish their studies and get down to serious business. The four

ALL OF RADIOHEAD'S AMBIGUITY IS EMBODIED IN THEIR SINGER AND THINKING SOUL, THOM YORKE

others are not just accompaniment. Through the years they've developed an extensive and subtle sound palette in which traditional rock instruments are combined with electronic textures and effects (effect pedals are Jonny Greenwood's specialty).

Intent on developing a personal lexicon, the group was sick of "Creep," a hit that was too basic for their ambitions. Following the success of that song, the five Oxford boys revealed their loathing, with Yorke singing in "My Iron Lung," "This is our new song/Just like the last one /A total waste of time." "Creep" was banned from their concert songlists for years, and when the following album *The Bends* was being made, it was a source of comparison. It wasn't until *OK Computer*, falsely pronounced commercial suicide because of its occasionally claustrophobic atmosphere, that Radiohead and their fans found themselves on the same wavelength. Although the group could have continued in the tradition of U2's epic rock, they instead borrowed and assimilated foreign elements from jazz and hip hop in an amazing maelstrom mastered by the producer Nigel Godrich, who became the equivalent of a sixth member. Even more

FORMED IN 1992

radical, *Kid A* also reflected a desire to reinvent themselves, guided by Yorke's whims. Weary of his fame and of burying his secrets discreetly in his lyrics, he preferred to hide behind the machines he tamed. Ever since, aside from lucrative tours, the group has spent its life in the studio, where they can experiment and where

SELECTED DISCOGRAPHY

OK Computer (1997)
The breakthrough album (their third). A totally ambitious and unique kind of rock.

Kid A (2000)
A staggering dive into electronic music that aged Britpop thirty years.

Hail to the Thief (2003)
A return to spontaneity and guitars, and hybrid compositions fueled by electro.

In Rainbows (2007)
The perfect synthesis, also available as a double-album.

A story by Morgan Navarro

PLAYLIST

1 Creep (1993)
2 High and Dry (1995)
3 Fake Plastic Trees (1995)
4 Just (1995)
5 My Iron Lung (1995)
6 Paranoid Android (1997)
7 Karma Police (1997)
8 Exit Music (1997)
9 No Surprises (1997)
10 Lucky (1997)
11 Everything in its Right Place (2000)
12 Idiotheque (2000)
13 Pyramid Song (2001)
14 I Might Be Wrong (2001)
15 Knives Out (2001)
16 2 + 2 = 5 (2003)
17 Where I End and You Begin (2003)
18 There There (2003)
19 15 Step (2007)
20 Reckoner (2007)

HEAD

hits from the outside cannot enter. Radiohead's influence cuts across genres: while many British rockers, from Muse to Cold War Kids, have seen the light in *OK Computer*, the jazz pianist Brad Mehldau, DJ Shadow, electro producers, and reggae artists (see the covers of *Radiohead* by Easy Star All-Stars) have also capitalized on the movement orchestrated by Yorke and Co.

In a rock scene that's obviously macho, the sudden emergence of Polly Jean Harvey in the early 1990s could have only been a feminist act, an aggressive statement about virility. Not only did she surface with a coarse-sounding album, but she clearly wasn't looking either to flirt with male fans, hurling raw and sexual lyrics at them. She grew up in the English countryside and shares a birthday with Margaret Thatcher (the resemblance stops there). Reluctantly, she developed a reputation as a suffragette, even as a castrating Amazonian—as if she had to play the part of watchdog because she was unwilling to reinforce male clichés. On her first two albums, *Dry* and *Rid of Me*, she crudely investigates the relationship between men and women, especially through the figures of Tarzan and Jane. She was revealing herself and literally stripping herself bare, unself-consciously, to the point that conservative critics saw her as provocative, as wanting to spark debate. Some fifteen years later, the misunderstanding has been partly cleared up: although Polly Jean still goes against the grain, her ambition has nothing to do with the war of the sexes. While Somerset's wild child has quieted down over the years, it's because she has tamed herself, gradually finding her own way toward peace and a form of happiness. Her fans in particular realized that they needed to distinguish her from the dark sensuality of her music.

Rejecting the image of a tortured artist with bleak thoughts, the English musician likes to think of herself as a storyteller. Like Nick Cave, with whom she has collaborated, she takes on the narrative tradition of the bluesmen that inspired her, as well as their sense of clever metaphor, which encompasses religion and sex. Even though her music is a more explosive approach to pure blues, sometimes verging on punk, she strives to find the same simplicity as Robert Johnson or John Lee Hooker, favoring warmth and the emotional power of homemade recordings over the coldness of high-tech productions. What guides her seems to be her search for the purest possible expression, whether she's drawing on an energetic guitar or less electric means (see, as early as 1993,

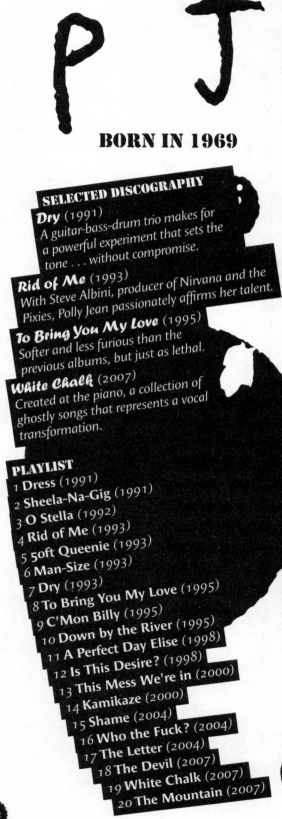

BORN IN 1969

SELECTED DISCOGRAPHY

Dry (1991)
A guitar-bass-drum trio makes for a powerful experiment that sets the tone . . . without compromise.

Rid of Me (1993)
With Steve Albini, producer of Nirvana and the Pixies, Polly Jean passionately affirms her talent.

To Bring You My Love (1995)
Softer and less furious than the previous albums, but just as lethal.

White Chalk (2007)
Created at the piano, a collection of ghostly songs that represents a vocal transformation.

PLAYLIST

1 **Dress** (1991)
2 **Sheela-Na-Gig** (1991)
3 **O Stella** (1992)
4 **Rid of Me** (1993)
5 **50ft Queenie** (1993)
6 **Man-Size** (1993)
7 **Dry** (1993)
8 **To Bring You My Love** (1995)
9 **C'Mon Billy** (1995)
10 **Down by the River** (1995)
11 **A Perfect Day Elise** (1998)
12 **Is This Desire?** (1998)
13 **This Mess We're in** (2000)
14 **Kamikaze** (2000)
15 **Shame** (2004)
16 **Who the Fuck?** (2004)
17 **The Letter** (2004)
18 **The Devil** (2007)
19 **White Chalk** (2007)
20 **The Mountain** (2007)

Harvey

A story by Fred Bernard

the sextet version of "Man-Size"). Not wanting to repeat herself on the deceivingly calm *White Chalk*, she turned to the piano, an instrument she is still far from mastering. This way she could drive away from the comfort of habit and set her inspiration free. At the same time, in order to retain a certain innocence, she used Post-its to remind her to sing . . . as if she were five years old. Hence the transformation on that radical album, a collection of dark tales that sound like an indie-rock version of *Wuthering Heights* or Faustian pacts; and the tour that followed, where she proudly stood alone onstage.

ALTHOUGH POLLY JEAN STILL GOES AGAINST THE GRAIN, HER AMBITION HAS NOTHING TO DO WITH THE WAR OF THE SEXES

Over the years, PJ—whose sensual charm Jean-Louis Murat has honored ("Polly Jean," on *Mustango*)—hasn't become conventional, she's still rebellious and dissatisfied. It makes sense that, drawing on the 1960s icon Marianne Faithfull and her freedom, she especially feels close, artistically speaking, to strong-willed musicians, from the prickly Tricky to Thom Yorke of Radiohead, from the French Pascal Comelade to the American Sparklehorse or the Icelandic Björk, who, like her, is always trying to reinvent herself. Polly Jean, like her elder Patti Smith in the 1970s, has truly inspired certain new female singers. But none has been able to imitate her or even pretend to be related. Ardently authentic and truly independent, Polly Jean Harvey prefers to live out of the spotlight and glitz in her native Somerset. That's where Fred Bernard goes to find her.

215

This just isn't right. I'm going crazy. What can I do?

At night, I dream of you. I wander among the wolves. What can I do?

Everything reminds me of you. Nothing interests me anymore. What can I do?

Coil the rope around my neck? Kiss yours, ever so softly? What can I do?

In hindsight, it's easy to say that everything in the life of Kurt Cobain, the singer and tortured soul of Nirvana, was leading up to the final crash of his suicide on April 5, 1994. On that day, he consciously staged his departure, leaving IDs on his breast before writing a farewell letter and shooting a bullet into his head. A month before, after a first failed attempt in Rome—he had ingested a champagne cocktail of tranquilizers—he scribbled an eloquent "fuck you" as he came out of his coma. His destiny was not that of an ordinary lost soul because he was able to channel his nihilism, his anger, and his profound distress into astounding songs. These touched an entire generation of young outsiders, for whom he became first a herald and then a martyr. The filmmaker Gus Van Sant drew heavily from his tragic end to make the movie *Last Days* in 2005; this wasn't unusual, after A. J. Schnack's documentary *About a Son*. You hear Cobain, interviewed by Azerrad,

KURT COBAIN WAS ABLE TO CHANNEL HIS NIHILISM, HIS ANGER, AND HIS PROFOUND DISTRESS INTO ASTOUNDING SONGS

remembering that as a child he thought he was an alien and that in school they thought he was different, even dangerous: "Others thought I was capable of coming to class with an AK47 to kill everyone." A statement that strangely echoed the massacre at Columbine, in Colorado, long after his death, and which inspired Van Sant to make *Elephant*. But, despite being harassed as a kid and despite early bouts with depression after his parents' divorce, Cobain only took his own life. His was saved for years when he discovered rock, the hard kind, like Led Zeppelin and Black Sabbath, then American hardcore (The Melvins, his favorite). But Cobain was never a purist, never only interested in a single genre: he respected obscure groups but also liked Kiss and the Beatles. The success of his songs stemmed from an explosive combination, a mix of rage and fragility, to which he succumbed. For behind the big sound and electric noise,

there are, indeed, melodies extracted from a pop context.
In terms of form, his songs had nothing to do with the structure of the blues either. But in spirit, they represented a contemporary, white, and despairing interpretation of the genre.

After recording with his first group—sarcastically named Fecal Matter, in 1985—Cobain met the bassist Krist Novoselic. In March 1988, they presented themselves for the first time as Nirvana, surely unaware that there was an English band of the same name in the 1960s. Cobain associated the notion of nirvana, especially used in Buddhism (where it means "salvation"), with his definition of punk rock as an open field. After *Bleach*, created with the first drummer Chad Channing for the label Sub Pop, which soon became the epicenter of the Seattle grunge scene, David Grohl joined the group in 1990.

A story by Guillaume Bouzard

NIRVANA

1988 – 1994

Then everything accelerated. On the recommendation of the singer from Sonic Youth, Nirvana signed with a major label (Geffen) and recorded *Nevermind*, a true instant classic, as Guillaume Bouzard recalls in the pages that follow. The formula, borrowed from the Pixies (Cobain was a big fan), was captivating, alternating noise and quiet. The success of the album stirred up a genuine revolution worldwide: alternative rock reached large audiences and many long-haired bands were brought out from the wings and into the spotlight. Thrust into celebrity at a time when he thought his life would not go beyond club concerts, Cobain found the attention difficult to bear. And this attention grew—exponentially—when he married the singer Courtney Love. They had a little girl together, but his wife's pregnancy (who reminded him of Nancy Sprungen, Sid Vicious' junky girlfriend) was disturbed by persistent rumors about their addiction. Cobain, who used to soothe his stomach with drugs, sunk into a deep depression that was accentuated by conflicts with his label over the relative drop in sales of *In Utero*. His suicide in April 1994 put an end to Nirvana, but the group's influence continues to be important. As for David Grohl, he has continued on in a similar vein (but this time as singer) as frontman of the Foo Fighters.

NiRVANA

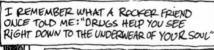

SMELLS LIKE TEEN SPIRIT...

GOOD GOD... IT REALLY GOT YOU GOING!

THREE HUNDRED MILES IN ONE SHOT, DUDES...

THE FOLLOWING WEEK, WE SPED OFF TO A FESTIVAL...

YEAH, BABY, ON THE ROAD AGAIN FOR ROCK.

RENNES 8

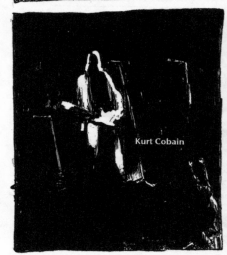

Jack White unquestionably perpetuates the spirit and authenticity of the blues, but he is a shrewd and unusual contemporary bluesman. This native of industrial Detroit has proved to be as comfortable with old classics, which he approaches credibly, as he is in our "society of spectacle," dominated by image and marketing. As if his heroes—John Lee Hooker, Robert Johnson, and Son House—had been resurrected in the body of a young white man who knew that in order to get his band out there and charm MTV, he needed to collaborate with Michel Gondry. He both respects traditions and has an innate ingenuity, a clash between rustic convictions (he was almost a priest) and an extremely sharp and modern vision of business. Of course, the success of the White Stripes can be explained by the fire of their steamy, heavy rock in the vein of AC/DC; by the solidity and appeal of their songs, which sound as if the Beatles were producing Zeppelin-like melodies. But the strong sense of identity they've promoted from the start, based on an untouchable color code—white, red, and some black for contrast—has helped popularize the duo. They've even declared the color combination to be the most powerful there ever was—from the Coke can to the Nazi flag. They're so interested in visual effectiveness and invention that they even named their album as part of the De Stijl artistic movement, to which Piet Mondrian belonged. A common devotion therefore brings together the bluesman Blind Willie McTell and Gerrit Rietveld, a designer whose work appears in their notes.

Born John Anthony Gillis, Jack has a sense of formula. The White Stripes' formula relies on a simple and minimal recipe characterized by the number 3; the sum of vocals, guitar, and drums represents the backbone of most of their songs. Championing the motto of the twentieth-century German architect Ludwig Mies Van der Rohe, "less is more," Jack's position has been to subtract rather than to add excessively. He's convinced we need restrictions to be free. In order to succeed, he needed a second half to lean on. This pillar would be the subtle Megan

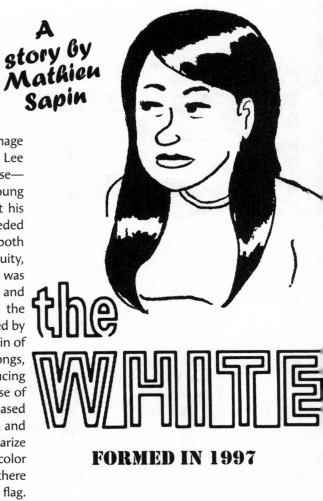

A story by Mathieu Sapin

the WHITE

FORMED IN 1997

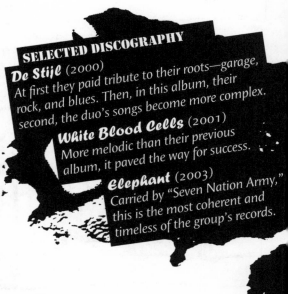

SELECTED DISCOGRAPHY

De Stijl (2000)
At first they paid tribute to their roots—garage, rock, and blues. Then, in this album, their second, the duo's songs become more complex.

White Blood Cells (2001)
More melodic than their previous album, it paved the way for success.

Elephant (2003)
Carried by "Seven Nation Army," this is the most coherent and timeless of the group's records.

Martha White, a true soul mate, to whom he was married for four years (they divorced in 2000). Then they presented themselves as members of the same family, a good trick. Like Moe Tucker, the female drummer for the Velvet Underground, Meg White, with her innocent looks, plays her rhythms in an original and raw way. Her ex describes it as caveman beating! Jack set out with her on a bold and paradoxical musical journey that defies convention while remaining familiar. The duo never even considered a third member, so

JACK WHITE IS A SHREWD AND UNUSUAL CONTEMPORARY BLUESMAN

STRIPES

that they could maintain their intimacy. (They chose to bypass the bass.) But they've patiently expanded their sound palette, introducing piano, or marimba sounds, even bagpipes and mariachi trumpets. Since 2006, Jack White has also been the frontman of a second group he formed with the singer Brendan Benson, the Raconteurs. But his ambition seems to be the same: mastering American blues and rock, as if it were his native tongue, paying tribute to Dylan as a god and father. He wants nothing other than to make his contribution to this collective body of work. He can already take pride in having composed "Seven Nation Army," a hit from 2003 that shook up his career. Mathieu Sapin was crazy about it. It has even been borrowed and remixed to become a soccer stadium chant.

PLAYLIST
1 The Big Three Killed My Baby (1999)
2 You're Pretty Good Looking (For a Girl) (2000)
3 Hello Operator (2000)
4 Apple Blossom (2000)
5 Death Letter (2000)
6 Truth Doesn't Make a Noise (2000)
7 Dead Leaves and the Dirty Ground (2001)
8 Hotel Yorba (2001)
9 I'm Finding It Harder to Be a Gentleman (2001)
10 Fell in Love with a Girl (2001)
11 Seven Nation Army (2003)
12 Black Math (2003)
13 I Just Don't Know What to Do with Myself (2003)
14 The Hardest Button to Button (2003)
15 Blue Orchid (2005)
16 My Doorbell (2005)
17 Forever for Her (Is Over for Me) (2005)
18 Icky Thump (2007)
19 You Don't Know What Love Is (You Just Do As You're Told) (2007)
20 Conquest (2007)

ZAMBUJEIRA DO MAR, PORTUGAL. SUDOESTE OPTIMUS Festival, in 2004.

a comic strip is BLACK, WHITE and RED!

BLACK
WHITE
RRRRRRRRRRR
RRRRRRRRRRR
RRRRRRRRRRR
RRRRRRRRRRR
RRRRRRRRRRR
RED

Jack and Meg WHITE come out onto a large stage flooded with screams and applause.

Jack tunes his guitar and Meg takes off her small sandals and sits at the drums.

The crowd pushes up against the stage. The band gets ready to play one of the most legendary concerts of their budding career.

Just one little idiot in the back leaves and heads toward the parking lot.

The concert ends. Meg and Jack WHITE walk off stage, leaving their fans with the memory of an historic concert.

The kind of concert you brag about years later to your grandchildren: "I was there."

But right now, our heroes are tired. They haul themselves into their red and white bus and drive into the night toward well-deserved sleep.

Oh Jack, look at this! An accident!!

I don't give a shit!

You're lucky to be alive. You didn't see the white stripes?

The WHITE STRIPES?

LATER, BACK IN PARIS.

TA-TATATA TA TA

The WHITE STRIPES? Of course I know them. I have all their records.

I even saw them in concert last summer. It was a crazy scene.

Look, I'm still wearing my cast.

L'ALHAMBRA STOOGES

FIN

231

lcd sound system

A story by Luz

FORMED IN 2002

"I'm losing my edge [. . .] But I was there/I was the first guy playing Daft Punk to rock kids/I played it at CBGB's/Everybody thought I was crazy/We all know/I was there/I was there/I've never been wrong." Right away with his first single, "I'm Losing My Edge," New Yorker James Murphy, the brains behind LCD Soundsystem, was ironically showing that he was no fool—the song is criticizing the absurd race to be a trendsetter. In a single song, reminiscent of Captain Beefheart, the Beach Boys, Lou Reed, Detroit techno, and a number of influential but little-known groups (Can or EG), he was making a personal confession. After forty years

of pop music and rock, it's impossible for the insatiable and indulgent James Murphy to enter into totally new and unknown ground, to invent something that is completely unrelated to his record collection. "Losing My Edge," for example, contains hints of the B-side of a Killing Joke record, that post-punk group from 1980. Realizing that he has to digest a history that, for the most part, has been written, Murphy has nevertheless been able to take this constraint in a fascinating direction that has a furiously contemporary style, perpetuating what Talking Heads had also understood in the late 1970s in New York—unlike those 20-year-old rockers

discover the disobedient power and energy of house (especially Daft Punk, a real reference for him). Rock was at an impasse, but the openness of club culture drove him into the heart of a New York movement where former punks like !!!, a.k.a. chk chk chk, had converted to dance. Co-founder with Tim Goldsworthy of DFA Records (Death From Above), Murphy, popular for his remixes, has launched rock groups like the Rapture and Radio 4. Like the Belgians of Soulwax, also known as 2 Many DJs, Murphy scouts out the immediate future of rock. Admitting that he's terrified of simplistic people, as a singer, he chases away cliché and isn't scared to take a stance (as in the song "North American Scum," which mocks primitive anti-American sentiment). He even wrote a love song to a city ("New York I Love You But You're Bringing Me Down"). Unlike the other writers in *Tunes*, who don't know their "subjects" personally, the artist Luz is—as he explains in the following pages—a friend of Murphy's. Their shared musical references make them part of the same family. We can't say he's objective.

IT'S IMPOSSIBLE FOR THE INSATIABLE AND INDULGENT JAMES MURPHY TO INVENT SOMETHING THAT IS COMPLETELY UNRELATED TO HIS RECORD COLLECTION

mimicking the Stones, the Beatles, or Led Zeppelin, as if their clock had stopped in the 1960s or 1970s. Encompassing the tension of deviant punk (the Fall, Gang of Four), mutant disco (Arthur Russell), Brian Eno's experimental pop, and even the repeating music of Steve Reich or Terry Riley, LCD Soundsystem represents the most persuasive attempt to invent a meta-rock, which looks back (just a little) in order to move forward. Tired of the complacency and narrowmindedness of independent groups in the 1990s ("It was so boring that I stopped playing music then"), Murphy was literally shocked—with help from uppers—to

235

PLEASE NOTE: YES, JAMES MURPHY AND I KNOW EACH OTHER A BIT... IN 2002, HIS FIRST SINGLE WAS RELEASED, "LOSING MY EDGE," WHICH I DEVOURED TO THE POINT OF WEARING IT DOWN.

THE FIRST LCD CONCERT AT THE TRANS FESTIVAL IN RENNES THAT SAME YEAR! SHOCK!

FEBRUARY 2005, I GIVE HIM MY FANZINES AND MY COMIC STRIP ON THE FALL AFTER A CONCERT IN PARIS ... AND A BOTTLE OF COUGH SYRUP...

THEN ONE DAY, A TEXT...

"HI LUZ! KNOW WHAT? I'M DRINKING BEER WITH YOUR MASTER MARK E. SMITH" "THX FOR YOUR SYRUP, IT WORKED!" "SEE YOU IN PARIS"

JUST AS OBSESSED WITH THE FALL, I WAS MORE JEALOUS OF MARK E. SMITH BECAUSE HE WAS DRINKING WITH MURPHY THAN THE OTHER WAY AROUND...

I'M GOING TO SAVE THIS TEXT UNTIL THE DAY I DIE!

I'VE LOST MY CELL FIVE TIMES SINCE...

THEN WE SAW EACH OTHER AGAIN AND FOUND OUT THAT WE HAD THE SAME DISCO-FRIENDLY PUNK PAST...

YOU'RE LIKE ME, MY FRIEND!

...WE WERE A BIT TRASHED THAT DAY, BUT IT STUCK:

SO, ON THE RARE OCCASION THAT HE'S IN PARIS, WE GO FOR A WALK AND TALK ...

WHEN I STARTED DFA, I DIDN'T HAVE AN APARTMENT, I WAS SLEEPING ON A COUCH IN THE OFFICE...

SOMETIMES I'D TAKE MYSELF TO A HOTEL TO SLEEP IN A REAL BED. ONE DAY, THE HOTEL OWNER ASKED ME IF I WANTED TO PLAY RECORDS FOR NEW YEAR'S, AND HOW MUCH DID I WANT TO GET PAID... "I WANT THREE MONTHS FREE IN THE HOTEL," I TOLD HIM... AFTER A FEW WEEKS, IT BECAME HOME: I'D WALK AROUND IN A BATHROBE AND KNEW THE NAME OF EVERY MAID!

HI JAMES!

HI KAREN!

IT'S JUST SNOBBERY WHEN AN ARTIST CLAIMS HE HATES HOTELS